STRUGGLE FOR HUMAN RIGHTS

STRUGGLE FOR HUMAN RIGHTS
Nelson Mandela

Meena Anand

Publications
KALPAZ PUBLICATIONS
DELHI - 110052

Struggle for Human Rights : Nelson Mandela

Rs. 690

ISBN : 81-7835-317-2

Published in 2004 in India by
Kalpaz Publications,
C-30, Satyawati Nagar,
Delhi-110 052
Email : kalpaz@hotmail.com

Laser type Setting by: Tact Computer Graphics, Delhi
Printed at: Mehra Offset Press, Delhi

Contents

Preface

The Present Work "Struggle for Human Rights: Nelson Mandela" is outcome of my independen research under the guidance of my supervisor.

I am gratefully to my supervisor Dr. Suresh Kumar, lecture in Deptt. of Africa studies, University of Delhi. I express my sincere thanks to my Madam Dr. Sargh Mirtra for her guidance is preparing this work. Her constructive criticism and valuable suggestions have refined my thinking and has resulted in the formulation of the present work.

I am thankful to Dr. Dharam Pal, Deptt. of African studies, University of Delhi for his good wishes and academic guidance given from time to time.

I deem it to be my paramount duty to express my sincere gratitude to my father Dr. Tej Singh, research scientist, Deptt of Hindi, University of Delhi, who encouraged and enlightened me throughout my research work. I am highly indebted to my mother Mrs. Vidya, who entended an unfailing enthusiam and monetary assistance that made me complete the course successfully in time. I am thankful to my grandmother Mrs. Ratni Devi for her insperation and blessing in my research work.

I am grateful to my brothers Sanjay, Shekher, Anil, Aloke and my bhabhi Hema, my sister Anita, Mamta, Kapil and Prem Anand, my nephew Manshu and Sambhav for giving me all the encouragement.

I am grateful to uncle Mr. Ram Lal, and aunty Mrs Savitri.

I am thankful to the library staff of Central Reference Libarery, Teen Murti, Sapru House, India Institute of Public Administration (IIPA) and Department Library for help and guidance to my friend Sangeeta, Preete, Dr. Garima, Vidushi, Medhavi.

Meena Anand

1
Introduction

Federalism, that is to say the constitutional distribution of power between a national government and a number of state or provincial governments, is particularly suitable for diverse societies such as Switzerland. It is also appropriate for large countries like the United States, Canada, and Australia, the other three "Classic" federal systems.[1] The federalism which inspired the American Constitution comprised a number of important principles that included not only the distribution of powers but other principles like the separation of powers and checks and balance.[2] Debate about the future forms of central, regional and local government in South Africa are, at this stage, both highly speculative and specific to each level.

Murray Forsyth, observations on the nature of federalism offer a useful point of departure, "The definition of federalism will always be difficult, but as a process it involves a movement to establishment a union between several states or state like bodies 'which sustains the statehood of the component unit while at the same time limiting it."[3] As a moment, federalism is thus not necessarily concerned only with sovereign states which 'come together' or with entities such as colonial possessions which are brought together. Federalism may equally receive its impetus from decentralising government, already in existence. It is important, too, to distinguish the federal state itself from a 'confederation', the letter is more than a more alliance because it entails a treaty based form of government enabling several states to exercise certain key policies in common, but it is too loose to be called a form of state.

The right of the component states may consist in a federation like :

– The basic right of guaranteed existence, so that they cannot be abolished without their consent.

– The right to an area of original legislative and administrative competence,usually embracing those aspects of government which directly effect the citizens daily personal existence,

– The right to participate in the exercise of power (mainly economic) of the federal state itself.[4]

Studies of the patterns of governance in advanced third world states indicate that often these are strong corporatist pressures at work, tending to lock government, business and organised labour into a close and indeed closed relationship. A primary concern is thus to service the relevant constituencies, unless there are countervailing (institutional) interests with political leverage. Federal devices can be of critical importance in such cases. Contrary to the prevailing conventional wisdom that federalism in the third world has been a 'dismal failure'. Ralph Lawrence contends that 'regional government' can be 'significant' in creating resources for economic and social development in the states that comprise the union.[5] While for some, the great attraction of federal proposals is to counteract the power of a unitary state, for others it is their gravest defect. Albee Sachs has expressed this perceptions with telling force' "Behind all, these devices are two fundamental principles there shall be no majority rule and there shall be no rapid moves to end the inequalities produced by apartheid."[6] And again : "for nearly eighty years, to quote the official motto, unitary has been strength. Only now that the prospect of universal suffrage is on the near horizon, does unity suddenly become weakness."[7]

Nevertheless, despite the ANC's insistent invocation of the principles of a unitary state, it is clear that the federal idea will be approached from a variety of directions in negotiations for the new Constitution. That idea will have considerably more appeal if federalism is seem to be not simply a defensive or reactionary stratagen but a device consonant with democratic aims, indeed, as a means to their realisation.

Federalism and South Africa

Federal schemes have a long tradition in South Africa's political history, and it is ironic that unlike so many of the other major pre-colonies of Britain (such as United States, Canada, India and Nigeria), South Africa opted for a unitary system in 1910. The National Party, which came into power in 1942, had changed the constitution tremendously.

The concept of federalism has a long history in the English-speaking reformist community. The Progressive Party (PFP) advocated a federal formula as far back as 1962, following the recommendation of its internal Motteno Commission (mainly for the whites). The United Party (UP) adopted a federal programme (again for the minority whites) in 1972, and its successor, the new Republic Party, has advocated a 'federal-confederal' option for South Africa.[8]

The Union has been sporadic revivals of federalist proposal and indeed from the 1970 onwards, they have been widely conversed. Developed in the 1970's as alternatives to apartheid, these ideas have been drawn on in various ways to fill the vacuum caused by the loss of faith in the ideology of apartheid and its failure in practice on the one hand and the pressure of armed struggle led by ANC on the others. Overall with a liberal perspective, the Progressive Party advanced complex and sophisticated proposals for a democratic non-discriminatory federal government states with proportional representation for groups associated on a Voluntary basis and enjoying rights of minority veto at vital levels of decisions-making. It is worth nothing that while the Progressive Federal Party initially advocated a qualified franchise, it adopted a policy of universal suffrage in 1978. Its successor the Democratic Party (DP) was of course committed to universal suffrage, which was conceived in purely geographic terms, and its borders had more explicity rejected the concept of groups as constitutional buildings blocks.[9]

Albie Sachs is no doubt correct in observing that the association with proposals for a qualified franchise contaminated the doctrine of federalism, as the federal concept thus came to be associated with the paternalistic notion that blacks were almost, but not quite good enough to take part in governing the country.[10]

The PFP and DP coupled federal proposals with the concept of a Bill of Rights and this could possibly after a point of contact for discussions within the ANC itself. A different emphasis was to be found in the proposals for a 'race relations' developed in the 1970's by the old United Party and its successor the new Republic Party. These ideas concerning 'corporate federalism' were in effect, taken over by the National Party in the tricameral Constitutional plan. The abolition of the Group Areas Act and the Population Registration Act established a new, unfamiliar and challenging content for the identification of significant groups and the possibilities of their accommodation in local, regional or central political structures.

The ideology of federalism not only did generate a considerable body of academic literature but more importantly, how the federal policies were practically implemented by the ruling party or policies is a matter of concern. Really, the whites (Political Parties) were anxious to limit the power of government and prepared to accept a gradualist approach even if only as a 'second best' (for blacks) especially as a way of re-attacking the homelands to South Africa."[11]

Race has finally jettisoned by the National Party as a criterion for the definition of groups and in 1970 and other apartheid policies gradually invoked. Overall, the gradual change in the

National Party (NP) government strategy, culminating under F.W. de Klerks's leadership in the unbanning of the ANC.

The ANC and the National Party appear to be in agreement as the desirability of longer, more effective local authorities, and stronger regional government based on units smaller than the present provinces. ANC favours greater regionalisation, it has also insisted, over the years that South Africa must be a unitary state. Dr. Zola Skweyiya the head of the ANC's Constitutional Department says, "while we reject federalism and decentralisation as a strategy to retain privilege, we see the need to create new forum of regional government which recognize and address the problem of apartheid settlement patterns and the current uneven development across the country."[12]

While the ANC is formally committed to the views that there should be no real autonomy or regional power for regions and local authorities or major issues, it proposes the delegation of power to these levels for the purpose of 'more efficient administration and democratic participation'. According to Dr. Skweyiya, local and regional government thus should be seemed as potential development agencies. As such they should be able to exercise some leverage over choices among competing priorities, "although the central government must have some control over the issues that are vital to the conduct of national policy and must ensure uniformity of standards."

It is significant that the ANCs consultative conference on local government, held in October1990, stressed the need for flexibility in the formulation of policy. The goals of such policy would be:

- to create the basis of the country's resignification by incorporating the Bantustans;
- to promote national reconciliation and establish the basis for a more just and equitable allocation of resources and rectify the legacy of apartheid;

– to foster economic growth, democratic government and empower communities; and

– to develop efficient and effective structures for planning and catering for rapid urban growth service delivery and support for smaller local authorities and rural areas.

By the end of 1990, the government according to the Deputy Minister of Constitutional Development was looking for a constitutional model 'which do two things satisfy democracy by giving everyone a vote of equal value and resolve the conflict or the potential for conflict'.[13] Representation and responsiveness had become the requirement to the diffusion of power and the dispersion of conflict. The federal forum which has particularly engaged the attention of Pretoria's Constitutional planners is according to reliable sources, that of the German Federal Republic– a markedly centralised system in adopting federal policy to local circumstances. The political authorities of the lander have also had an institutionalised role in the federal government, through their representation in the Bundesrat, which is unparalleled in any English-speaking federation. The lander have an institutional say too in sharing out the total fiscal cake, with fixed shares in the proceeds of major taxes, while the appointment of a further block of taxation is subject to the assert of the Bundesrat. According to Dr. Meyar however, the government was not looking at any particular model.[14]

The independent South Africa after its first election was governed by an interim constitution that embodied many democratic features - with the aid of the tenure of the government of national unity in 1999 the society also became committed to endue further towards a more permanent and comprehensive democratic system.[15]

1. The Constitution of South Africa shall provide for the establishment of one sovereign state, a common South African citizenship and a democratic system of government committed to adjoining equality between men and women and people of all races.

2. Everyone shall enjoy all universally accepted fundamental rights, freedoms and civil liberties.

3. The Constitution shall be the Supreme law of the land. It shall be binding on all organs of state at all levels of government.

4. There shall be a separation of powers between the legislative, executive and judiciary with appropriate checks and balances to ensure accountability, responsiveness and openness.

5. There shall be representative government embracing multiparty democracy, regular elections, universal adult suffrage, a common voter's roll and in general, proportional representation.

6. Government shall be structures at national, provincial and local levels.

Historical Background of Human Rights in South Africa

The period of 1910 to 1948 : the rise and fall of the first centre coalition

The Republic of South Africa as it exists today is the result of a long and complicated process of interaction between African people and Dutch and British, colonists who came to exploit the territory. The original cape colony was settled by the Dutch in the 17th century but felt into British hands as result of the Nepolean war. Discontented Boers, or Afrikaners tracked northward in 1835-1837, commencing a half-century subjugation of the Zulu and other native people and establishing the independent republics of Transvaal and organge free state. The discovery of diamonds and gold in the late nineteenth century, the two Boer republics were captured by Britain in the Anglo Boer War of 1899-1902.

On 31 May 1910 four British dependencies were emerged to form the Union of South Africa, a dominion under the British

Crown. The first break in party structures came in 1910 when Hertzog with his orange free state following from the South African Party to form the National Party (NP) under wealth this split were two related issues. The first was the language question, with Hertzog demanding compulsory in structure in both official languages (English and Africana) in the schools. The second was the issue of national versus imperial loyalties and interests. Hertzog was always prepared to regard as South Africans or 'Afrikaners'? And his 'two-stream' policy fully recognized the cultural rights of the English. More the less, he had become an embarrassment to P.W. Botha in his dealings with the English in the government.[16]

The white worker labour party won the 1924 parliamentary elections. Under the new government 'civilized labour' policy, blacks were removed from many jobs to be replaced by whites. It also legislated for racial job reservation. The NP was now realigned with the South African Party (SAP), emerged victorious from parliamentary elections held in 1933, after which the two parties formally merged as the United Party (UP) Hertzog, the Prime Minister, was then able, with sinuts assistance to remove black voters from the Cape electoral roll. A small group of extreme Afrikaner nationalist MP's under Daniel Malan, formed the 'farified' MP which drew substantial support from the Broderband.

The segregation in the form of apartheid had consisted two main elements of negative and positive nature. The former drew the fear of the whites of being outvoted by the numerically superior Black population. This fear was assuaged by legislative terminating any possible extension of the long standing non-racial franchise in the cape to the rest of the union. The Black in the cape, which was only province in which they enjoyed the franchise, were taken off the common electoral roll and transferred to a separate roll to elect three white representations to the house of Assembly. In the rest of the union where, blacks were given four Representation in the senate.

In addition to this union, wide natives Representatives Council was established based on partly elective and partly appointed, which was to be regularly consulted about all legislation concerning Blacks. The positive elements of the segregation policy was conceived curiously as a quid proque for removing the Blacks in the cape itself from the common roll, which as the debates on the legislative concerned showed was not lightly entertained.[17]

The outbreak of the Second World War in 1939 split the UP because smuts supported the war a small majority for participation on the Allied side, white Hertzog and some of his followers went into pre-war economic depression, began to revive and demanded the implementation of democratic reforms including universal suffrage. African trade unionism expanded and a well organised union established itself among. African mine workers on the Rand. Although Smuts reflected the ANC's political proposal and used armed force to suppress a black mine-worker's strike in 1946, the UP began to adopt marginally more liberal attitudes in the immediate post war period, accepting the need for increasing African Urbanization and some liberalization of racial criteria in job reservation.

Expressions of Black protest not to mention the complications of the Indian problem in Natal for the united party, were readily exploited as campaign issues by the Nationalist.[18]

Yet in 1948 they polled only a minority of the popular vote, and were aided in their parliamentary representation by Smuts had been advised to change. They did not even win a parliamentary majority. At that moment the majority of South African people were gearing for a leadership which could bud the country together. What was needed was nothing less than for Smuts and N.C. Havenga to abandon party identities, draw up a programme of principle, the care of would be 'the building up and expansion of western civilization in South Africa'. Dr. E.G. Malharbe spelled out the following key point in this programme :

(a) "co-operation between the English and Afrikaners speaking sections;

(b) the economic development of South Africa in agriculture and industry;

(c) a programme immigration policy not only to build up the numbers of the whites race, but also because too desperately need trained people to realize.

(d) The maintenance of our democratic way of life and the combating of Fasicism; whether in the form of Broederbond.Gestapo government or in the form of totalitarian communism."[19]

The Centre Overpower

South Africa joined with Britain in both World Wars, its British common wealth attachments progressively weakened as the result of widespread anti British sentenioned and racial preoccupations.[20] In the mean time the concept of apartheid as we know it was introduced in South Africa after the Nationalist victory in the 1948 elections. Robert Price argues that in pursuing apartheid the National Party had three aims :

1. "to create a completely segregated society in keeping with the precept of Afrikaner politico-religious doctrine, and in so doing preserve - Afrikaner politico-religious doctrine, and in so doing preserve - Afrikaner identity;

2. to serve white political supremacy and its resulting economic privileges from potential internal and external threats;

3. to remove the Afrikaner community into a position of social and economic party with the English speaking community, which had dominated the modern economy and urban sector since the down of capitalist economic development in South Africa.[21]

The basic aims of apartheid South Africa's domestic strategy have been consisted from the 1948 to 1990. The apartheid become official government policy in 1948, when the Afrikaner National Party won the general elections, so bringing with it institutionalized racial domination, in all spheres of life - political, economic and social. The National Party government quickly began to setup a legal framework to discriminate against Black South Africans. In 1949 and 1950, the Prohibition of Mixed Marriages Act and the Impartiality Act forbade interracial marriage and sex. Other restrictive laws of 1950 were the politically repressive suppression of Communist Act, the population Registration Act which would underpin the racial classification so critical to apartheid's logic and functioning and the Group Areas Act, which required the racial segregation of residential and business areas. A number of laws were passed preventing black people from using the same public facilities as whites. Fundamentally, the Bantu Education Act did away with most mission schools, which were more independent and in their place instituted government syllabi designed to train blacks to be little more than minimally skilled labourers for white economic gain. The instruments for political repression also become stranger with apartheid's passage in response to the growing resistance of Black South African.[22]

Indeed, resistance to racism, exploitation and political repression were seldom for behind the laws and actions that defined the National Party's apartheid rule.[23] The members of the African elite in 1912, under the chairmanship of Pimely Seme, established the South African Native National Congress, soon renamed the African National Congress (ANC). Earlier Mahatma Gandhi first employed the technique of passive resistance against discriminatory legislative affecting South African Indians. Winning limited concessions he bequeathed the models of passive resistance to future protest-movements against racism in South Africa.[24] The ANC together with coloured, Indian white and communist allies, become increasingly militant in the 1950's, as the Congress and its allies started to use techniques like civil disobedience to resist white rule. The Sharpeville incident of 1960, in which police shot dead 69 people who were protesting against the Pass laws, in a protest organized by the Pan Africanist Congress (PAC), a resistance organization that had split from the ANC. The government then banned the ANC and PAC and in turn both organizations turned to violent protest through the ANC's armed wing, 'Umokhanto We Sizwe'.[25]

The government was largely successful in crushing resistance to its rule in the 1960's, and a climate of fear permeated South African life until 1976, effectively dissuading most people from activism and protest. In 1976 school children in Soweto, the black township outside Johannesburg, reflected the Afrikaans language requirement forced upon them, and began a protest movement that with landsight, was a turning point towards the end of apartheid.

The Soweto uprisings and the brutal suppression by the government quickly had a domino effect of resistance by students around the country. Thousands of students went into exile, mainly to join the banned ANC and its guerrilla army, although the PAC, many countries, and universities around the world, were also recipients of the exiles. Hundreds of youth, and many older people who worked with them were sent to prison, for charges ranging from public violence to terrorism. The prisons, and in particular Robben Island which already housed the 1960's generation of political activists, were in turn used as universities of politics; in which the ideologies and strategies of challenging apartheid were endlessly debated, to ensure released political prisoners could reengage the apartheid state, with over greater sophistication.

Prime Minister Verwoerd was assassinated by a deranged while man in September 1966, but his successor, Bathozer J. Vosster, continued Verwoerd's policies, bringing to fruition the ideas of separately the Blacks into separate tribal homelands, or "Bautustans". These areas encompassing approximately 13 per cent of the country's land, were ultimately intended to house upwards of three-quarters of the population. Concurrently, a series of minor concessions to the Blacks brought about a challenge from the right wing, or Verkrampte (unenlightened) factions of the National Party under the leadership of Dr. Albert Hertzog who formed the National Party (HNP) to compile in the 1970 elections.[26] The NP easily by-passed his challenge, the HNP winning no legislative seats on a 3.56 per cent vote share, although the opposition United Party (UP) made some gains. At the next parliamentary elections in April 1974 the NP increased its majority, the UP lost five seats and the Progressive Party (PP) managed to get only a single seat.

The oppression of white government turned hostile and in 1975 number of people died in the 'Church Massacre Incident' in Soweto. Subsequently, the white government introduced "Afrikaaner" as official language and medium of teaching in the schools and other education institutions. In response to that, the black movement turned aggressive and in 16 June 1976 police opened fire against the the innocent school children in which number of people were killed in Soweto (Mandela government inaugurated a "Peace Pole" in the memory of the people in 1996).

Human Rights in 1980 to 1999

The beginning of the 1980's South Africa was widely predicted to be an route to a bloodbath, whose apartheid legacy would be a black versus white civil war. At the very least, the country was at an impasse. The political settlement and endemic violence were accompanied by worsening poverty and a declining economy, which had been damaged by international sanctions the costs of enforcing apartheid in South Africa.[27]

The course of South Africa's history was changed, however, when on February 2, 1990, the New President, FW de Klerk, announced that the ANC and its ally, the SACP, the PAC and the other banned organizations were to be unbanned and Nelson Mandela was to be released. The announcement inaugurated the process of end of apartheid rule, and the beginning of a process that would involve four years of negotiations that would set the stage for the country's first democratic, participatory and non-racial election. A snap shot summary of the four years transition is worthwhile. Between February 1990 and December 1991, the transition was by comparatively little in the way of formal negotiations. The ANC announced a ceasefire in the armed struggle, a January 1991 agreement between Mandela and Buthelezi to end violence between their supporters; and the National Peace Accord was signed in September 19991 by all major political grouping.[28]

The first full-fledged negotiating forum, which the major political parties joined at its inauguration, was the convention for a Democratic South Africa (CODESA), which was intended to begin negotiating the new constitution. The Conservative Party and other right wing groups, the Azanian People's Organization (AZAPO) and the PAC were absent during the negotiations of CODESA. Although the Inkatha Freedom Party (IFP) did attend, its delegation was not led by Buthelezi who refused to attend unless the Zulu King, King Goodwill Zurlithini, and a representation of the Kwa Zulu government were invited together with an IFP emissary. This was the beginning of a pattern, for Buthelezi, was the only political leader in South Africa never to attend any session of the negotiating conventions.[29]

A few months after CODESA was converted, a referendum was called by the National Party government for March 1992 to obtain a mandate for its political initiatives. Although they received their mandate in part due to the support of their negotiating partners, their success lured them into an exaggerated sense of control, and the National Party began to make unrealistic demands in the negotiating process particularly in demanding 75 per cent majorities to adopt certain key decisions.[30]

In June 1992, armed Zulus from a local hostel massacred local residents in the townships of Boipatong. This was not the first or last massacre, but it was the catalyst to the ANC, calling off negotiations in CODESA. The residents believed that the police were implicated and assisted the IFP in its attack. It was not an isolated perception "there was an absolute conviction in the minds of nearly the whole black community government plot to weaken the ANC and its supporters".[31] The impasse in negotiations and the frustration of the ANC's constituency, led the ANC to walk out of CODESA.

Ironically it was another incident of violence that led to talks being resumed although private negotiation and discussions had never ended at senior levels in the ANC and NP. As part of the ANC's 'rolling mass action' compaign launched in the wake of CODESA's failure. The ANC decided to challenge the homeland or bantustan governments. The perilous nature of violence was underscored; and the political settlement were hurting the economy and the society as a whole. Mandela reduced the ANC demands and de Klerk responded. Formal negotiations were resumed once more.

The previous negotiations had broken down in significant part because the NP wanted a power-sharing formula of government that would avoid the loss of power involved in the majority rule democracy that the ANC sought a compromise solution was proposed by Joe Slovo, the white communist party chairperson, writing in the African Communist in 1992. Slovo argued that because the ANC was not dealing with a defeated economy; it had to make certain concessions to first achieve an agreement that would facilitate a constitution and election, and second, ensure that a new ANC government would have the bureaucratic and institutional levers of power at its disposal.[32] The ANC could offer the NP limited but compulsory power sharing a government of national unity, a general amnesty, and security to the predominantly white civil service.[33] Thus in February the following years, the NP and the ANC proposed power sharing and an interim government of National unity for five years after the first democratic election.

The sense of betrayal experienced by Buthelezi and the IFP was evident in the failure of government attempts to talk to IFP in October, and rather democratically, in the format of the right wing alliance with the IFP, certain homeland government, and Afrikaner political organizations. This Coalition of the Concerned South African

Group (COSAG) which was later renamed the Freedom Alliance, opposed the domination of the ANC and NP in the negotiation process. By April 1993 multiparty negotiation resumed, and included twenty six parties covering much of the South African political spectrum. The country was governed by the Transitional Executive Council representing different political parties but primarily the ANC and National Party government till the first democratic elections.

The central parliament was to comprise a house of assembly of 400 members, all elected by proportional representation but on a basis of one-half from national and one-half from regional list. The national and regional assemblies and governments were to functions within the limitations of a justifiable interim bill of rights. The interim parliament was to subsist for a maximum of five years. The forum did not succeed in winning the assent of Buthlezi, the Afrikaner Volks fronts and the representatives of Boputhantswana and the askei. They now formed a new alliance namely the Freedom Front (FF) which threatened to boycott the April 1994 election. On May 1994 the national assembly elected Nelson Mandela as president. In accordance with the interim constitution, an interim government of national unity was formed in which the ANC, the DP and IFP were represented in proportion to the number of seats that they had won in the election. Thabo Mbeki and de Klerk both became deputy president. In accordance with the interim constitution, all former 'homelands' were reincorporated into South Africa, which was henceforth divided into the nine provinces, each with its own legislative and executive. The interim government of national unity focused on the maintenance of stability and the promotion of economic growth with initial emphasis laid on a Reconstruction and Development Programme (RDP). The installation of a democratic government, South Africa was admitted into the OAU, the common wealth and the SADC, and resumed its seats in the general assembly of the UN.

References

1. Dougles V., Verney and Balveer Arora, *Multiparty identities in single state: Indian Federalism in Comparative Perspective* (Delhi, Konark Publishers, 1995), p. 1.
2. Dougles, *op. cit.*, p. 2.
3. Mcoray Foryth's, *Federalism and the future of South Africa* (Johnnesburg, South African Institute of International Affair, 1989), p. 40.
4. Dougles Irvine, "Federalism and the New Constitution" in Alexender Jonston, Sipho Shezi and Cavin Brodshow, eds., *Constitution Making in the New South Africa* (London, Leicortes University Press, 1993), p. 13.
5. Dougles, *op. cit.*, p. 6.
6. A. Salchen, *Protecting Human Rights in a South Africa* (Capetown,Oxford University Press, 1990), p. 4.
7. A. Sachen, Ibid, p. 151.
8. Philip Frankel, *State Resistances and Change in South Africa* (London, Croom Helm, 1989), p. 37.
9. "South African Institute of Race Relation", 1990, Race Relation Survey 1989/1990, SAIRR (Johnnesburg), p. 703.
10. A. Saclm, *op. cit.*, p. 17.
11. Dougles Irwin, *op. cit.*, p. 17.
12. David Tucker, "Some Reflection on the Interim Constitutional Arrangement" in Paul B. Rich, ed., *Reaction and Renewal in South Africa* (London, Macmillan Press, 1947), p. 73.
13. *Ibid*, p. 79.
14. Report on the ANC national Consultative Conference on local government a discussion, Betvilla, Centre for Development Studies, University Press of Western Cape (UWC), 1990 (1).
15. Dougles Iruine, *op. cit.*, p. 43.
16. David Tucker, *op. cit.*, p. 74.

17. Erich A. Walker, *A History of Southern Africa* (London, Longman Publisher, 1964), p. 546.

18. South of the Sahara, 1996, p. 860.

19. Howard Brotz, *The Politics of South Africa* (London, Oxford University Press, 1977), p. 11.

20. Kenneth A. Heard, *General Election in South Africa 1943-1976* (London, Oxford University Press), pp. 237-45.

21. Jean Van Ber Poel, Selections from the Smuts Papers, Vol.III (Cambridge, Cambridge University Press, 1973), pp. 237-45.

22. Howard Brotz, *op. cit.*, p. 26.

23. M. Robert, *The Apartheid State in Crises : Political Transformation in South Africa, 1975-1990* (New York, Oxford University Press, 1991), p. 19.

24. John Mukum Mbaku and Julies O. Thomson, "South Africa's first democratic elections and their political content" ed. In *Multiparty Democracy and Political Change* (England, Ashgate Publishing Ltd. 1998), p. 242.

25. John *op. cit.*, p. 243.

26. T. Hodge, *Black Polition in South Africa since 1945* (Ravan Press, Johannesburg, 1945), pp. 241-46.

27. Encyclopedia of Government, 1999, p. 862.

28. From Bunlman, "South Africa's First Democratic Elections and their Political Content" in John Mbaku and Jolius O. Ihmobere, eds:, *Multiparty Democracy and Political Change : Constraints to Democratizations in Africa* (England Ashgati, 1998), p. 848.

29. P. Grastow, *Bargaining for Peace : South Africa and the National Peace Accord*, (Washington, DC, 1995), p. 23.

30. A. Sparks, *Tomorrow in Another Country : The Inside Story of South Africa's Negotiated Revolution* (Sandtorm, Strink Brook Distribution, 1994), pp. 130-132.

31. From Bustrman *op. cit.*, p. 249.

32. A. Sparkes, *op. cit.*, p. 4.

33. *Ibid*, pp. 180-82.

2

Human Rights : Theoretical Perspectives

In the modern democratic world the relation between the man and the state is determined by the extent to which the man is provided with liberty, equality, justice and rights in a society.

The first and foremost issue is that of human rights. The medieval period witnessed bloodshed because of the defence of the religion and established order. But in our age, there are revolutions and national movements for rights, liberty, justice etc., and almost every social issue of our age is associated with any of them. The main slogan of liberal philosophy has been 'rights' – of property, equality, religion, speech etc. The basis of the power of the state is mainly its capacity to ensure rights. Thus, the question of rights is one of the fundamental questions in the social and political thinking of our age.

Rights are the necessary conditions for the personal, social, economic, political, mental and moral development of man but are necessary for the development of society and social values as well. Rights are the social requirement of a social man for the development of his personality and society at large. Thus there are two aspects of rights social and personal. Rights of the individual are merely antisocial privileges if these are a hindrance to social development. Rights have a social character and are given only to the man living the society and working in the overall interest of the society. Rights cannot have anti-social nature because no rights can be permitted to the individual at the cost of social well being.

The Concept of Rights

Being a crucial concept, Rights have been defined differently by different writers. Laski has defined rights as, "those conditions of social life without which no man can seek, in general, to be at his best."[1] T.H. Green defines right as power of acting for his own ends... secured to an individual by the community on the supposition that it contributes to the good of the community.[2] According to Barker, "Rights are the external conditions necessary for the greatest possible development of the capacities of the personality"[3] Salmond has defined a legal right as "an interest recognized and protected by a rule of law - an interest the violation of which would be a legal wrong... and respect for which is a legal duty."[4]

From the analysis of these definitions we may infer that Rights are the demands of an individual from society for the development of his self. When society concedes these demands then these become rights. Secondly, Rights are given only to the social individual; thus rights do not originate outside the society. Thirdly, rights are restricted for social interest and welfare. But the basis of imposing restrictions should be reasonable. Fourthly, Rights ought to have a moral basis and should be given equally to all individuals of society. Fifthly, state is not the creator of rights, but merely its servant and guardian. And lastly, rights and duties are correlated. The rights of an individual become the duties of all the other individuals of the society.

Though there is a general consensus among the social and political thinkers on these characteristics of the rights, but during the course of development, various theories of rights have emerged. These theories can be analysed as under:

Theory of Natural Rights

This theory of rights was propagated by liberal thinkers during the early phase of liberalism, in the 17th and 18th century. The main contention of this theory is that each individual has some natural, inalienable, fundamental, inherent, absolute, sacred human rights by birth itself. These rights can neither be taken away by any other individual nor be restricted by any authority and these are independent of society and the State. All these natural rights are pre-colonial and pre-social, and must be recognized in every socio-economic, political, legal and moral system. For this theory, the natural rights are an end in themselves.

John Locke strongly supported the theory of natural rights. Among these he counts right to life, liberty and property as the most important.

Though this theory of rights have been criticised on the grounds of being ambiguous and against equality, it can be safely said that this theory played an important role against the absolutism represented by kings, papacy and feudalism. Though rejected in our times, this theory in its spirit still exert considerable influence. The fundamental rights incorporated in the constitution-both of liberal and socialist countries-are its living monuments.

Legal Theory of Rights

This theory developed from the logical necessity of protection and recognition of natural rights of the individual. Thomas Hobbes was the first to propound this theory. It was further developed by Austin and Bentham. This theory refuses to accept that rights are created by nature as it maintains that the origin of rights lies in their recognition and protection by the laws of the State.

Legal theory of rights entrusts three functions to the State. Firstly, to determine the rights; secondly, to define the scope of rights; and thirdly, to remove the hindrances which come in the way of the fulfillment of rights.

Idealist theory of Rights

The third phase of the development of the concept of rights can be said to be the phase of moral rights. The theory of moral rights has been supported by the French philosopher Rousseau, German philosopher Kant and English philosopher T. H. Green.

According to this theory, no individual can have any right against the common interest of the society and against moral values. Rights are not rights either because they are natural or because they are legal, they are rights because they have a moral value and a moral object. The object of rights is not to serve the selfish interest of an individual, but to help his moral uplift. Rights are given to the social man as the necessary external conditions for his moral and social development. This aspect of rights is an important basis of the theories of rights in the 20th century.

Historical Theory of Rights

Thinkers of the historical school maintain that laws are a product of long historical evolutions of a society and are based on traditions, customs and demands. They further hold that with the change in time and circumstances rights also change. Rights are the crystallization of customs and traditions.

Supporters of the historical theory of rights are Savigny, Ranke, Burgess and Maine. These thinkers were jurists and were raising their voice of protest against natural and positive schools. They maintained that as the character of laws was historical so also was the character of rights.

Social Welfare Theory of Rights

The main contention of this theory is that individual rights are limited by social welfare. Rights are not given to anti-social individuals and rights are always restricted in the interest of the society. Individuals are given rights so that they may contribute to the common good. An individual who does not perform his social function and does not contribute to common welfare cannot claim any rights. This theory emphasises the social character of rights.

The concept of social welfare was recognised by J. S. Mill and subsequent liberal thinkers like Cole, Hobhouse, Barker, Laski and Tawney.

Marxist Theory of Rights

All the above theories represent the liberal concept of rights. According to the Marxist theory. Rights are the product of class struggle in particular historical circumstances. These are the achievements of bourgeois revolution and were used by the emerging capitalist class against the feudal privileges and against the absolutist monarchies. This theory holds that rights have a social character and in order to be real, the condition of their realization must be provided by society. Each person should contribute to society according to his ability and each should get from the society according to his needs.

Marxist theory gives more importance to social and economic rights such as rights to work, education, social security, rest and adequate wages. Apart from rights, socialist States also mention some duties of their citizens, i.e., obedience to laws, constitution and rules of the socialist society; performance of the public functions with honesty; protection of socialist property; duty of serving in army; ensuring security of the country.

Though above theories are different from each other and some of them are contradictory as well, but now in the era of democratic socialism and welfare state this is a generally acceptable view that rights are the sum total of those opportunities which ensure enrichment of human personality and these can be safeguarded by the rule of law, separation of powers, independence of judiciary, written constitution and limited government.

Development of Human Rights

Ever since the emergence of the civil society, the issue of individual rights has been a central question of social and political sciences. Though human rights have made their appearance in positive law at a late date in the history of civilisation and the ancient system of law didn't know human rights as we conceive them now, the western world did make some progress under the cannons of the Roman Church. But there was no systematic theory of rights even during the Roman or Greek period.

We may find some developments in the history of international law as far as the phenomena of human rights is concerned. In 1555 the freedom of religion was pledged by the Christian European states in the 'Treaty of Augsberg'. Certain degree of freedom was again guaranteed by the 'Treaty of Westfalia' in 1648. The 'Vienna Congress' of 1815 laid down several provisions of human rights. The 'Paris Treaty' of 1856, the 'Berlin Treaty' of 1878 and the Paris Treaty of 1898 made provisions regarding the protection of human rights.

The demand for individual rights is associated with the rise of modern period. During the medieval period, the idea was that every man had its appointed role, function and status in a pre-established order. The concept of rights emerged in modern times, out of the criticism of the existing order.

Historically, the demand for individual rights was made by the rising commercial middle class, which was the product of industrial revolution. It was the accepted ideology of American and French revolutions and was expressed in the American Declaration of Independence in 1776 and in the Constitutional Bill of Rights and in the Declaration of the Rights of Man in France in 1789 French Revolution gave the slogans of "Liberty, Equality and Fraternity." The Glorious Revolution of 1688 in England gave the right of representation to the common people. Prominent liberal thinkers such as John Locke, Rousseau, Bentham, J.S. Mill and T.H. Green supported the rights of the human being on one ground or the other.

To emphasize the importance of rights adjectives such as 'natural,' 'fundamental' and 'human' have been used in the long history of their development. With the enormous expansion in the wealth and expectations the list of these rights have tended to be lengthen. Men have become more aware of how one, another live, not only between country and country, but also between continent and continent. The sense that poverty, disease and ignorance need not to be the inevitable lot of most of world's inhabitants and that these could be remedied by deliberate action, has led to the recognition of certain economic and social conditions as 'human rights'. Law of the state, morality, social, political and ideological values and socio-economic system gave substance to the human rights.

The concept of human rights has become increasingly important in liberal democratic world as well as in the socialist countries and the third world. The period following the Second World War has witnessed an unprecedented debate on, and concern for human rights both at national and international levels. Human rights are currently a matter of international interest and concern for a wide variety of reasons[5].

With the emergence of nation states and establishment of despotic regimes towards the close of middle ages, the struggle for the rights of man started, originally, within the national boundaries. As a reaction to the authoritative and repressive regimes, history witnessed the great political revolutions of the late seventeenth and eighteenth centuries. The phrases of human rights which had, at that time, been abused were formulated into declarations and bills of rights and were written subsequently in national constitutions.

The pace of history has since been greatly accelerated with the incredible advance in science and technology. Mass media of communications and the lightning means of transport have levelled the national barriers, transforming the one time unknown and mysterious tracts into a close and familiar habitat of mankind. The man-to-man contact has changed the very ecology of international life and the everyday shrinking distance has brought the human miseries in distant lands close to our doors.

The rapid industrialization and the demands for higher standards of living have added to the complexities of present day societies. No nation today is, in a true sense independent; no country, however large and powerful, is sufficient into itself; no country, however small and unobtrusive, can live much less thrive, in isolation. The increasing interdependence of modern world – economically, strategically, culturally, politically and technologically – has made concern for human rights 'a major international fact.'[6]

The more immediate reasons for the genesis of international concern for human rights were, however born out of the events connected with the origin and conduct of Second World War. The war, fiercest in human history, brought in its wake not only infinite misery and devastation, but also manifested the inadequacies of rules of traditional international law to develop doctrines and procedures for protecting the individual from his own government. Nonetheless it awakened the world to the futility of entrusting the protection of human rights solely to the internal jurisdiction of nation state. The war resulted in a widespread conviction that the effective international protection of human rights was a major deterrent of the war inasmuch as it is an essential condition of international peace and progress. This faith was given repeated expression in several Allied official pronouncements and declarations which emphasized importance of the individual and his rights.

Because of the above mentioned reasons, a new wave of interest towards the rights of human beings was visible at the national and international levels. New areas were explored to make human rights more substantive and universal. At present, the human rights phenomena covers a much wider area. There are three generations of human rights, which are civil and political rights; economic and social rights; and cultural and educational rights. Civil and political rights made their appearance much earlier and economic, social and cultural rights followed much later.

Civil and political rights include right to self determination, right to freedom of expression, freedom from torture and inhuman treatment, freedom from slavery and forced labour, right to liberty and security, freedom of movement and choice of residence, right to fair trial, right to privacy, freedom of thought, conscience and religion, freedom of opinion etc. Economic, social and cultural rights embrace right to work, right to just conditions of work, right to fair remuneration, right to an adequate standard of living, right to organise, form and join trade unions, right to collective bargaining, the right to equal pay for equal work, the right to social security and the right to property, the right to education and the right to participate in cultural life and to enjoy the benefits of scientific progress[7]

Now, during the last two decades a new right, 'the right to development' has been discovered, which is considered a specifically African contribution to the international human rights discourse. According to the International Commission of Jurists Draft, the right to development is a right of individuals, groups, peoples and States to participate in and benefit from the process of development, aimed at realising the full potentialities of each person in harmony with the community. This right applies at all levels, community, local, national, regional and global.[8]

This is evident from the above discussion that the concept of human rights has come a long way and several new additions have also been made. Though there could be different views over the prioritization, but generally all the above mentioned rights are accepted as essential and necessary for the human development, in nearly all the societies and states.

Scope of Human Rights

Despite ever increasing tensions within several differing areas of the globe, in the post cold war period there has come to be a general acceptance of the universality of human rights. But mere acceptance or theoretical conceptualization is not enough for rights to be actual and this doesn't assure the security of a person's or group's or nation's fundamental rights. Hence, an authorized machinery or institution should be given the responsibility, not only to define and explain the nature of rights but also to act accordingly for their protection and promotion.

Human Rights Protection at the Global Level

At the global level the protection of oppressed or endangered groups by international treaty started in the seventeenth and eighteenth centuries in matter of religious liberty. In the course of the nineteenth century the international treaty was used to protect ethnic and racial groups and to combat the slave trade and slavery; in the twentieth century it has been used to improve labour conditions, to arrange for the supervision of the administration of mandated territories, and to provide under the supervision of the League of Nations for certain rights of social, religious or linguistic minorities in a number of states, mainly central and eastern Europe.

Not until the world had passed through the tragic events of World War II and had witnessed the barbarous acts committed by the totalitarian regimes of that period, was the universal organizations of the international community, the United Nations, charged with some responsibilities in the matter of human rights, and its members pledged themselves to take actions for the achievement of universal respect for and observance of human rights and fundamental freedoms for all. The San Francisco Charter of 1945 through which the peoples of the United Nations reaffirmed their faith in "fundamental human rights" didn't define these rights. The Charter has made it abundantly clear, however, that one particular activity atleast is repugnant to it: discrimination on the grounds of race, sex, language, or religion.

Nor has the Charter established specific international machinery for the enforcement of its human rights provisions, except for arrangements under the trusteeship system. But it has created organs of general and wide competence—the General Assembly, the Security Council and the Economic and Social Council—and it has laid the foundations for the establishment of an unlimited number of subsidiary bodies, including Commissions in the field of human rights.

The General Assembly, and to some extent also the Economic and Social Council, have not hesitated to use their general powers of investigation and recommendation to take action of varying character and intensity in such situations as violations of religious or political freedom in Eastern Europe, race conflict in South Africa, forced labour in various parts of the world, infringement of trade union freedom, practice violating the human dignity of women in less developed communities, the status of Budhists in South Vietnam, and many others. The fight against colonialism has been one of the characteristics of the international scene in the post-World War II world. The majority of governments have, to a large extent, identified the struggle against colonial domination with the struggle for human rights.

International Bill of Rights

Since the United Nations Charter had not defined human rights and had not created special international institutions for their enforcement, it was widely assumed in 1945 that this would soon be done in an 'International bill of rights'. In 1947-48 it was decided that this 'bill' would consist of two or more documents : a declaration, a convenient, and 'measures of implementation'. In 1948 the General Assembly proclaimed in a resolution the first part of this bill of rights as the Universal Declaration of Human Rights.[9]

The Universal Declaration of 1948 is the only worldwide official document where the human rights, of which the Charter speaks, are set forth. Its range is very wide. It proclaims not only the traditional, political and civil rights and freedoms of its national predecessors but also 'economic, social and cultural rights.' The declaration has, to some extent, filled the gap created by the delay in completing the covenants on civil and political; and economic, social and cultural rights. It has acquired a status, different from and more important than the one which was originally intended for it. It has been used by the United Nations, by other international organizations and conferences, and by governments, as a yardstick to measure the compliance by governments with the obligations deriving from the Charter in matters of the human rights. It has penetrated into international conventions, national constitutions and legislation, and even in isolated cases, into court proceedings.[10]

The main burden of implementation of human rights was, however, placed on Human Rights Covenants. The Covenant on Economic, Social and Cultural Rights carries a rudimentary form of implementation in recognition of the fact that these rights are in a stage of progressive development and can only be achieved progressively. The Covenant on Civil and Political Rights and the Optional Protocol attached to it include, comparatively, more comprehensive provisions on implementation of rights provided there in. The Covenant goes beyond placing general obligation on State party to the Covenant and designates a special organ of implementation the Human Rights Committee, composed of eighteen persons, to give effect to its provisions.[11] The Covenant requires State Parties to submit reports to Human Rights committee on the measures they have adopted, which give effect to the rights recognised and on the progress made in the enjoyment of these rights. The Committee was also given with the power to create a Human Rights Commission in this regard.

The contribution of the world body has been significant towards formulation of substantive law norms. It has kept the question of human rights in the focus of world publicity throughout by various means. By initiating the process of periodic reports from states, by providing advisory services to the needy governments, by compiling studies of specific rights or groups of rights, by offering fellowships to individuals and more particularly by debating the gross violations of human rights, the United Nations put flesh upon the bare bones on the human rights provisions of the Charter.

Besides United Nations, some International Non-Governmental Organization, such as International Committee of Red Cross (I.C.R.C.), International Commission of Jurists and Amnesty International have also played crucial role in the process of protection and promotion of human rights.

Human Rights at the National Level

While the concern of international community to deal with the crisis situations involving gross inhumanity shall manifest itself, in whatever measure, through the global organization on human rights, the wider task of implementing international human rights standards, by determining individual claims and satisfying them, should fall under national jurisdiction.[12] For the protection of human rights at the national level, several provisions have been made in various countries. Countries like France, have adopted and accepted fundamental human rights and have given them place in their declarations of freedom. Some other countries such as India, have included sets of rights in the constitutions of the state. In some of the countries, like in America, bills of rights have been added by constitutional amendments.

Nearly every state in the world today has provisions in its constitution or in the basic law for the protection of Human Rights and fundamental freedoms. This is particularly true of the countries which adopted their basic legal texts after the proclamation of the Universal Declaration of Human Rights in 1948; in some cases certain, or all, of the provisions of the declaration were incorporated in those texts. Citizens of such states who feel that they have been denied a right or freedom set out in the constitution or basic law may take their complaint to local or national administrative or judicial officials and seek a remedy of the wrong, allegedly done to them.[13]

Another suggestion which has been offered to protect human rights at the national level is to create an international machinery within nation states. The international agency may provide the states with a 'standard organizational framework' for adoption in accordance with their constitutional processes. The institution, however, should be established on the initiative of nation states themselves in accordance with their constitutional provisions and should purely be a domestic organ for implementation of international human rights standards. The functioning of national and international institutions side by side within their defined spheres of competence would combine in itself the twin element of centrality and locality. National Commission of Human Rights, functioning in each state can be a very useful tool in the global process of implementation of human rights and will serve as a safety valve before a situation explodes inviting international attention.

But no national machinery, established for the safeguarding of human rights, can be expected to operate satisfactorily unless it is supported by an informed and effective indigenous public opinion. Proliferation of non-governmental organizations formed on the initiative of people themselves, and encouraged by national and international action, appears to be the only way to involve each and every human being in the world movement of human rights. These bodies, like friend in need, will remain within walking distance from him on whose support he can rely for taking up his just cause and help him seek effective redress. Nongovernmental organization are thus the extreme manifestation of environmental implementation of human rights. There usefulness is borne out by experience in as much as the contemporary movement on human rights not only originated in non-governmental organizations, but owes most of its presently dimension to their initiative, exertion and endeavours.[14]

Human Rights at the Regional Level

The two-tier implementation at global and national level does not exhaust the possibilities of contemplated action on human rights. Still another manifestation of such an action can be through regional groupings of states. Regional arrangements and agencies manifest a natural growth of international co-operation and are desirable stepping stones towards world organization.[15]

The global and regional systems of the human rights should be co-ordinated and adequate measures for the harmonization of the two systems should be worked out. Regional organizations may be permitted a free hand in dealing with human rights problems in the areas where such areas are Voluntarily established. More particularly regional organs would be in a better position, in view of their vicinity, to supervise the international obligations which the states undertake in the field of human rights. The regional agencies may also involve themselves with such infractions as are not global in dimension.

In the years during which the United Nation had been slowly working its way toward the completion of the world-wide covenants, much more rapid progress was achieved in western Europe. Under the auspices of the Council of Europe, the European Convention of Human Rights of 1950 came into being, supplemented by protocols of 1952 and 1963 and by the European Social Charter of 1961. By the Convention, the 15 European states which are parties to it have undertaken to secure to every one, within their jurisdiction, the rights which it defines. The Convention established two new organs to ensure the observances of the engagements undertaken by the parties: the European Commission on Human Rights and the European Court of Human Rights. Western Europe remains a singular example where almost immediately after founding a political union, a very elaborate regional mechanism, providing for individual petitions and adjudications was instituted for protection of human rights. But the conditions in other parts of the world do not favour such a highly formalized structure to support the rights and freedoms of an individual. After a long hesitation, the Organization of American States could prepare itself for constituting just a study groups on human rights in 1959; and thus was born the Inter-American Commission on Human Rights. This Commission, in the course of time, set the tone for extending regional action on human rights in other parts of the world. The Organization of African Unity, encouraged by the American experience, adopted a 'Charter on Human and Peoples' Rights in 1981 which establishes an eleven member Commission and vests it with almost the similar mandate as envisaged for the Inter American Commission. The Banjul Charter also incorporates human duties and peoples' rights alongwith human rights.

Although the South Asian Nations have grouped themselves into a political union (SAARC) in 1983, they have yet to agree on some form of co-operation in the field of human rights. The region has gone through a harrowing experience of abuse of human rights. The people of Bangladesh still remain deprived of their hard won freedom. The curse of fear and want continues to afflict their lives even two decades after their so-called liberation. In other countries of South Asia also there are human problems which call for some dispassionate and humanistic handling by rising above narrow and selfish national interests as well as those of the ruling elite. It is, thus in the interest of South Asian Governments and their managers as well to institute a sort of SAARC Commission on the lines of Inter-American Commission to forewarn and possibly save them of the impending disasters.

In modern era, when the world is shrinking at an accelerating rate and moving towards the globalization, it is necessary to develop a new approach towards human rights and their protection. Though all the three levels and mechanisms of human rights work relatively independently from each other, even then it is necessary to co-ordinate the efforts made on all levels and certain degree of armonization is also required to exploit the potentialities of these mechanisms

Human Rights in Africa

In the post Second World War period few paradoxes are more disheartening than the proliferation of international human rights instruments on one hand, and the actual level of observance and enforcement of these norms, on the other.

Observance of human rights poses problems everywhere, and no country's record, be it highly industrialised or economically underdeveloped, is faultless. In most of the countries which have acceded to independence only in the recent decades, the problems are aggravated. Many of these countries have implacable enemies : poverty, ignorance, disease and inertia. At the Kabul conference it was agreed that there could be no meaningful exercise of human rights in a country where economic resources were scarce and the bulk of the population lived on the margin of subsistence.

Developing countries experience difficulties not only in regard to economic and social rights, the enjoyment of which clearly presupposes a certain economic standard, but also in regard to 'classical' civil and political rights.

The African continent, which had been under colonial rule until the sixth decade of the nineteenth century and where few countries have got their independence very recently also is not an exception. The history of African countries is strewn with the gross violations of human rights, and the situation is not that better even now. But before discussing the present state of human rights in Africa, it is better to take a cognizance of the African perspective of human rights. It is notable that human rights are conceived here as a pattern of personal security and the emergence and legitimization of fair judgements on particular issues,[16] which is a result of the violent changes and authoritative and totalitarian state activities, which the African continent had gone through.

Culture, traditions, customary law and moral values play dominant role in the conceptualization of human rights in Africa. Because of these factors, two streams have been created on the issue of the concept and nature of human rights in Africa. The first one believes in the universality of human rights on the grounds that, as human being, each person is entitled to certain human rights, which are part of the fundamental values that all cultures share. This view further maintains that there is a set of certain basic and fundamental rights, which should be restored and given to the person of each society, be it underdeveloped or highly developed. Like in any other country, the people of African countries should also enjoy their individual rights.

The other view which has been regarded as 'cultural specificity view' maintains that Africans have their own rich heritage and traditions of rights inherent within the community which is drawn, although not exclusively, from traditional African society.[17] As Rhoda Howard notes, such a claim is based on the communitarian ideal in which group is more important than the individual, decisions are made by consensus rather than by competition, and economic surpluses are generated and disposed of on a redistributive rather than profit oriented basis.[18]

In Africa it is argued that human rights as conceived in the West are rejected in the third world and in Africa precisely, because their philosophical bases are not only different but indeed opposite. Whereas Western conceptions are based on the autonomous individual, African conception does not know such individualism.[19] Vincent, Donelly and Howard have propounded an 'African Notion of human rights', which includes the following assumptions. First, they assert that human rights derive directly from a person's humanity. Their source is the best side of man's moral nature. Rooted in this nature that all human beings share, human rights are by implication inalienable, relatively absolute, and universal in scope and application. Second, they argue that human rights uphold human dignity but that these are by no means synonymous... Human rights are claimed rights or moral entitlements, not simply duties reciprocal obligations, or benefits. Third, Howard and Donelly assume the interdependence and equivalence of different kinds or generations of human rights. However, Howard argues that the pursuit of civil and political rights cannot be postponed until the achievement of social and economic rights, or indeed of women's rights or rights to development or group solidarity. Finally, they agree that because rights derive from human nature, they must inhere in individuals and in our mutual needs to live meaningful life.[20]

Though there isn't consensus on the nature of 'Notion of Human Rights' in Africa, but it is clear that, unlike that which some Western thinkers believe, there have always been some human rights' notion in Africa, though it is arguable, whether, there has been any codification, classification or institutional framework for their protection.

The state of human rights in Africa has never been satisfactory. But it is believed that pre-colonial Africans clearly recognised and claimed right to life, to liberty, to justice, to marry and have family, to freedom of speech, conscience and association, to participate in political process, and to freedom from poverty. But not all pre-colonial African societies claimed or observed these basic humans rights. The fundamental human right–the right to life was often violated at the time of war and conflicts. The practice of human sacrifice was another such exception. But the most obvious way in which pre-colonial African societies curtailed personal freedom was through the institution of slavery. In fact in diverse societies, in pre-colonial Africa, the rights which people claimed and the extent to which they exercised the rights varied enormously.

Under the colonial domination African societies became subject to political, economic and social domination, the African law ceased to be endogenously developed. The deculturization paved the way for the imposition of European education and values. Capitalist modes of production were also introduced which created elite classes and led to the alienation of the elite from the African masses.[21]

There is no doubt that by abolishing certain objectionable practices prevalent in traditional African societies - slavery, human sacrifice etc., the colonialists have contributed to a progressive development of human rights, but equally on balance there is no argument as to the fundamental negative effects of colonialism on colonial and independent Africa. Colonialism was essentially antithetical to human rights protection and promotion. Under the guise of civilizing missions, colonial powers systematically impinged upon every vestige of African life denying the African humanity itself.[22]

The history of most of the post-independence African states is filled with several instances of gross violations of human rights. Although at independence most of the states inherited a multi-party system, this was however quickly dismantled to give way to one party systems or military dictatorships, which was accompanied by violent suppression of opposition elements. The experience of supposedly multiparty states has not been very different either. Mass arrests, detentions without trials for long periods of time, mock trials and secret execution of opposition elements have been commonplace in Sekou Toure's Guinea; Egypt, Sudan, and Zaire, according to Amnesty report, to name a few, have been guilty of these crimes.

In most of the African countries, freedom of press and speech as well as freedom of assembly are enshrined in their constitutions. In practice however, these fundamental rights are denied to the people. Newspapers are in most cases government owned and only reflect government opinion. The perennial problem of military coups in Africa has also compounded the problem of human rights violations. Military coups have been followed by gross violations of the political and civil rights of the erstwhile rulers and their supporters. For example, the aftermath of first Jerry Rawlings coup in Ghana in June 1979 saw the swift execution of three former heads of state without proper judicial procedure. Apart from this, relations between most African States are far from cordial. Border disputes abound, allegations of one state harbouring and financing subversive elements against another are numerous. Coups, civil wars, tribal conflicts and social upheavals, prevalent underdevelopment, sporadic clashes between erstwhile hostile ethnic groups, low level of literacy and education, contradiction between the African customary law or Islamic law and imposed foreign legal systems blocked the road to the attainment of true and substantive human rights. Abject poverty coupled with growing population leave the vast majority of people of the continent without basic needs fulfilled. These challenges render the new states extremely fragile which limits the extent to which human rights can possibly be enjoyed by the people.

Because of some political developments and changes in the social and international environment, African peoples have become much more conscious about their fundamental freedoms and rights. With the fall of several authoritarian regimes, for example, in Uganda and Zambia, and pursuit towards democratic political systems, the environment is becoming much more conducive for the protection and development of human rights. Political developments are also paving the way for economic development. Earlier people, who were object of development, had to remain silent but now with the emergence of democratic societies people themselves have become the ends, not merely means; and with the access to the freedom of speech and expression, people are fighting with the ignorance, poverty and disease.

Earlier, right from the time of independence struggle, African leaders emphasized the importance of universal human rights and this commitment was further reaffirmed in the constitutions of their countries. The nature and content of human rights promoted and protected depended by and large, on their colonial experiences, there concrete material conditions and their ideological orientations. Countries of the capitalist orientations which were influenced by the *Judaeo Grecco Jurisprudence* adopted civil and political rights to the neglect of socio-economic rights. On the other hand, countries of socialist orientation sought to promote socio-economic rights, and adopted laws and measures to undermine capitalism.[23]

Despite these measures, and efforts made by some of the African leaders, the overall situation of human rights in Africa remained far from satisfactory. Because of the inadequacies of the national systems for the protection of human rights, African countries have accepted obligations under various international instruments that have laid down universal human rights standards. As long as they dealt with matters such as apartheid, colonialism and refugees, they were more inclined to comply. These countries have also accepted the supervision of United Nations in these fields, but when they touched on the activities of the modern states such as those that deal with matters of constitution, administration, justice and police, which are concerned with fundamental functions of the state, there was an obvious reluctance to accept international supervision and enforcement.[24]

However, efforts were made to create and African institution for promotion and protection of human rights at the regional level. The Organization of African Unity (OAU) has, since its inception, remained the focal point for the regional promotion and protection of human rights in Africa. In this regard, it has either acted alone or in collaboration with other international organizations such as United Nations and Economic Commission for Africa (E.C.A.).

The Organization of African Unity, which was established on the 25th May in 1963, was based on the fundamental principle of the 'Unity and Solidarity' of African people. The Organization, being the only one, of which all the African countries are members,[25] is the only institution on which they can rely upon for the protection of human rights. In the period of thirty six year the Organization has made several efforts in this regard. The role of the OAU, in the promotion and protection of human rights, should be assessed in all its manifestations–civil, political, social, economic and cultural. The potential of the OAU has to be assessed bearing in the mind that when the African governments, which have the primary responsibility to guarantee human rights within their domains, have fallen below the mark, whether the OAU can provide needed respite....In effect the acid test for the performance of the OAU in the field of human rights, goes beyond its efforts in the field of the fight against colonialism, racism and apartheid which are matters normally regarded as being outside the domestic jurisdiction of member states and should concern itself with the extent to which it has influenced and will continue to have impact on the fundamental functions of the governments, that is those of law making, interpretation and enforcement of human rights' laws and the creation of the socioeconomic conditions that give them substance[26].

The Assessment

One of the significant aspects of contemporary international relations is the importance, now being attached to the promotion and protection of human rights. But the situation had not been the same in preceding periods. The concept of human rights has gone through a process of development in which three generations of the rights have been emerged. But all around us is the stark reality of disregard for fundamental freedoms and human rights. The African continent has also been one of the most horrible examples of human rights violation. But keeping with the times African nations have chosen to accept, though partially, international supervision at the regional level, for the protection of the rights.

In this regard the Organization of African Unity has been aware and active since its inception in the year 1963. But to analyse OAU's role and actual contribution in the field of protection and promotion of human rights in the African continent, one must take a cognizance of the Organization itself, first. The need and the prevailing conditions which gave birth to the Organization, the background in which the Organization was established, the objectives, principles and the policies of the Organization are also worth studying. Because a fair analysis, a balanced evaluation and the prospects of the OAU in the field of human rights can be calculated only after that.

References

1. H. J. Laski, *A Grammar of Politics* (London, Penguin, 1925), p. 91.
2. T. H. Green, *Lectures on the Principles of Political Obligation* (London, Oxford University Press 1895), p.20.
3. E. Barker, *Principles of Social and Political Theory* (London, Penguin, 1951), p. 130.
4. P. J. Fitzerald, *Salmond on Jurisprudence* (London, Penguin, 1966), p. 218.
5. S. L. Bhalla, *Human Rights : An Institutional Framework for Implementation* (Delhi, Docta Shelf Publication, 1991), p. 1.

6. Ibid., pp. 2-3.

7. Osita C. Eze, *Human Rights, in Africa: Some Selected Problems* (Lagos, Mcmillan, 1984), pp. 5-6.

8. Issa G. Shivji, *The Concept of Human Rights in Africa* (Dakar, Codesaria, 1989), pp. 31-32.

9. *Encyclopeadea of Social Sciences*, Vol. III, 1979, pp. 541-42.

10. *Ibid.*, p. 542.

11. International Covenant on Civil and Political Rights, artical 2, clauses 1&2.

12. S. L. Bhalla, op.cit., p. 169.

13. *Ibid.*, p. 217.

14. S.R. Sharma, *Encyclopeadea of Human Rights*, Vol. III, (New Delhi, Rima Publishing House, 1996), pp. 279-80.

15. S. L. Bhalla, *op.cit.*, pp. 216-17.

16. Ronald Cohen, "Prolegomena to the Study of Human Rights in Africa", in Ronald Cohen, et.al. eds., *Human Rights and Governance in Africa* (Florida, University Press of Florida, 1993), p. 11.

17. Pal Ahluwalia, "Human Rights in Africa: A Post Colonial Perspective", *Africa Quarterly* (New Delhi), Vol. 38, No.1, 1998, pp. 23-24.

18. Rhoda Howard, "Is there an African Concept of Human Rights?" in R. J. Vincent, ed., *Foreign Policy and Human Rights* (Cambridge, Cambridge University Press, 1986), 27.

19. Issa G Shivji, *The Concept of Human Rights in Africa, op.cit.*, p. 12.

20. Tymothy Frenyhough, "Human Rights in Precolonial Africa," Ronald Cohen, et.al. eds., *Human Rights and Governance in Africa, op.cit.*, pp. 41-42.

21. Osita C. Eza, *op.cit.*, p. 9.

22. Pal Ahluwalia, *op.cit.*, p. 24.

23. Osita C. Eze, "The Organization of African Unity and Human Rights: Twenty Five Years and After", *Nigerian Journal of International Affairs* (Lagos), Vol.14, No. 1, 1988, pp. 157-58.

24. Osita C. Eze, *Human Rights in Africa: Some Selected Problems, op. cit.*, p. 11.

25. Except Morocco who withdrew in 1985 in protest against the admission of SADR.

26. Osita C. Eze, "The Organization of African Unity and Human Rights: Twenty Five Years and After," *op.cit.*, p. 155.

3
Human Rights and Political Parties

Political parties are essential features of the modern state and are critical forces in democratic countries. Parties in liberal democracies tend to play an integrated role, which bring people into the political process and provide channels of communication between society and political representatives. The political parties increase the legitimacy of political system. By building links with the public and articulating certain moral and social values and which can reduce the possibilities of violent outbursts. The political party has been regarded as 'critical force for modernisation', which can assist in the construction of new political institutions.[1]

Once formal independence had been achieved, however parties would be obliged to face the problems and demands of that society. It is the representative government of single or multi parties which initiates to solve these problems. Mostly, the newly independent government persuades the process of development in terms of social and economic upliftment and national unity.

The State of South Africa has been passing through the process of democratization both in political and in the economic spheres. The process of democratization should be incorporates the elements like pattern of government and multiparty system influences the process of development. Several formal and informal institutions play their respective roles in it. But political parties, undoubtedly, are the most crucial institutions which play central and significant role in this process. There are many political parties in South Africa who directly influences the political process of democratization. South Africa consists of multiparty system and the number of representative parties like African National Congress (ANC), Democratic Party (DP), New National Party (NNP), Inkatha Freedom Party (IFP), South African Communist Party (SACP), Pan-Africanist Congress (PAC), Azanian People's Organization (AZAPO), Freedom Front (FF), United Democratic Movement (UDM), and African Christian Democratic Party (ACDP) are playing an important role in the nation-building.

To understand the process of democratization in South Africa and to evaluate respective role of the political parties, it is necessary to take a cognizance into the emergence and development of different parties in South Africa and to analyze their manifestos and political programmes to find out their views on federalism and human rights.

Human Rights and Role of ANC (African National Congress)

The African National Congress was formed in 1912 and known as South Africa Native National Congress (SANNC). The task of the ANC after it was unbanned in 1990 was to change from being a liberation movement to a political party.[2] The ANC evaluates and reconsider its own organizational structure and constitution in the new South Africa. The ANC National Congress elected Nelson Mandela as president in 1991 and by 1994 the 49th National Conference amended and adopted a new constitution.[3]

The amended Constitution was intended 'to orient the structure of the organisation to conditions in the country since the 27 April (1994) elections' The main amendments regarded the structures of the organization and their functioning. The references to ''Umkhonto We Sizwe" were removed from existing

Constitutions and the National Defence Force integrated into the new South African. This Constitution describes the ANC as a champion of liberation movement which dedicated to the achievement of a united, non-racial, non-sexist, democratic South Africa. The Constitution outlines a framework for democratic, decision-making and accountable government

Constitutional developments and ideological dimension of African National Congress (ANC)

The African National Congress envisages a united democratic, non-racial and non-sexist South Africa, a unitary state where a Bill of Rights, guarantees of fundamental rights and freedom for all on an equal basis. The indigenous people lines on an open and tolerant society, where the organs of government are representative competent and fair in their functioning. The opportunities are progressively and rapidly expended to ensure that all may line under condition of dignity and equality. There are some features inherits in the Constitution for a democratic South Africa is as follows :

1. "To unite all the people of South Africa, Africans in particular, for the complete liberation of the country from all forms of discrimination and national oppression.
2. To end apartheid in all its forms and transform South Africa as rapidly as possible into a united, non-racial, non-sexist and democratic country based on the principles of freedom charter.
3. To defend the democratic gains the people and to advance towards a society in which the government is freely chosen by the people according to the principles of universal suffrage on a common voters role.
4. To fight for social justice and to eliminate the vast inequalities created by apartheid and the system of oppression.
5. To build a South African nation with a common patriotism and loyalty in which the cultural, linguistic and religious diversity of the people is recognised.

6. To promote economic development for the benefit of all.
7. To support and advance the cause of national liberation, women's emancipation, development, world peace, disarmament and respect of the environment.
8. To support and promote the struggle the rights of children."[4]

ANC supports unitary system and does not very much in favour of federalism. Though, the government claims to be a unitary state but it reflects the features of a federal state. The Constitution clearly demonstrate the division of power in each sphere of government which again strengthen the idea of federal state.

Constitutional developments and ideological dimension of African National Congress (ANC)

There are some features inherits in the constitution for a democratic South Africa is as follows:

A United South Africa

When we speak of a United South Africa, we have in mind in the first place the territorial unit and constitutional integrity of our country. South Africa must be seen, an recognised by the international community; as a single, non-fragmented entity including Transkei , Bophutatswana Venda and Ciskei. Secondly we envisage a single, citizenship, nation and a common loyalty.

Thirdly, all apartheid structure must be dismantled and replaced by institution of government–central, regional and local–which are truly non-racial and democratic.

Fourthly, there must be a single system of fundamental rights guaranteed or an equal basis for all through the length and breadth of the country. Every south Africa, irrespective of race, colour, language, gender, status, sexual orientation or creed should know that his or her basic rights and freedom are guaranteed by the constitution and enforceable by recourse to law.

Fifthly, the flag, names, public holidays and symbols of our country should encourage a sense of shared south Africanness. A unified South Africa requires a strong and effective parliament capable of dealing with the great tasks of reconstruction. All such governmental structures and institutions shall be based on democratic principle, popular participation, accountability and accessibility.

The new constitution must consistently and clearly affirm the fundamental principle of equal and undifferentiated citizenship so that the differences of culture, interest and personality can then express themselves in a constructive, free and non-conflictual way.

Democratic South Africa

The government must be democratic in the universally accepted meaning of the terms. It must be the government of the people, by the people, for the people. It must be chosen by the people in free, fair and regular election must be based on the principle of universal and equal suffrage on a common voters roll without distinction as to race, language, creed, class social position, birth or gender. The African National Congress favours the system of proportional representation, with regional and national list.

The legislature should be representative of the people as a whole, reflecting such differences of political views and interests as may be present in the community at any particular time.

The government must be open. Apartheid South Africa has been a highly authoritarian society, characterized by arbitrary decision making by officials and by excessive secrecy. All South African have the right to be informed about the issues and to know what the basis of governmental decision is.

Government should be based on the principle of active involvement of the people. The existence of civic associations, religious bodies, rate payers organizations, trade unions and other independent bodies should be encouraged. Similarly, governments should collaborate with non–governmental organisations, without interfacing with their autonomy. Government should reflect the will of the majority, be effective but not all powerful. It should operate within the framework of the constitution acknowledging a separation of power and the existence of fundamental rights and freedom as guaranteed in a Bill of Rights.

Non-Racial South Africa

A non-racial South Africa means a south Africa in which all the artificial barriers and assumptions which kept people apart and maintained domination, are removed. In its negative sense non-racial means the elimination of all colour bars. It positive means the affirmation of equal rights for all. It presupposes a South Africa in which every individual has an equal chance, irrespective of his or her birth or colour. Its recognizes the worth of each individual.

Non-sexist

The African National Congress believed that the new constitution must reflect a commitment to full, free and equal participation in the New South Africa. Law and practice keep South African woman out of their rightful place in helping to build democracy and enable a new nation to evolve and deprive them of their human rights as individuals.

The New Constitution must therefore:

guarantee equal rights for woman and men in all spheres of public and private life;

create mechanism whereby the discriminative, disabilities and disadvantage to which woman have been subjected are rapidly removed;

give appropriate recognition to reproductive and birth rights; guarantee constitutional protection against sexual violence, abuse harassment or defamation ensure that woman are heared in all issues and participate actively in all levels of society.

Bill of Rights

A Bill of Rights based on universally recognized principle of human rights should form an integral part of the New constitution.

In particular, it should guarantee all South African against the violations of human rights associated with apartheid stress the principle of the equal dignity and worth of all South Africans of.

The Bill of Rights should in clear and unambiguous language guarantee the rights of personal freedom and political expression. It should also protect and enchance rights of the individual to practice her or his religion and culture and speak her or his language.

All discriminatory legislation and all other legislation inconsistent with the Bill of Rights will be invalidated by the Bill of Rights. All other legislation will remain in force unless repealed by parliament or set aside by a court under its power of judicial review.

The state shall take all reasonable and necessary steps to protect, promote and enchance the language right of all the people of South Africa in relation to education and culture and in the functioning of the State at local, regional and national levels.

The language policy of the state shall be directed towards promoting and encouraging multilingualism and preventing the use of any language or languages for the purpose of domination or division.

The question may, of course, be asked whether there should be one official language for the country. But if this choice is made it would mean the demotion of some language or the promotion of a single one. Also it could mean that the official language would be one which most of the people either do not speak or do not speak fluently.

There will be a public service commission changed with the responsibility of overseeing the recruitment, promotion and dismissal to and from posts in the civil service. Such a commission will also be required to implement an affirmative action programme in regard to appointment to senior position in order to redress existing race and gender disparities. Provisions will be made for a representative structuring of the public service, the police service and defence service and to ensure that the public service will be accountable for its actions.

There will be an independent Ombud with power to investigate complaints against member of the public services including the police and other holders of public and private power and to investigate allegation of corruption. The constitution will also make provision for a state of emergency to be declared when the life of the nations in threatened. Such a power will be subject to strict controls by parliament and the judiciary. The constitution will provide for the recognition and protection as far as possible of fundamental rights during the periods of emergency.

The constitution will be subject to amendment only if a majority of two thirds of the national assembly approve of the amendment or if approved by two thirds of the votes cast at a national referendum.

All South African shall be entitled to stand for election as president, to parliament and to other elected offices. Election will be supervised by an independent electoral Commission and conducted in accordance to with the standards designed to ensure that the elections one fair and free.

All languages of South Africa will have equal status. They will be set out in a schedule to the constitution and will include in alphabetical order the following. Afcikaan English, Sipedi, Sesoth, Seswati, Tronga, Tswana, Vendo, Xhosa Zulu.

Human Rights and National Party's (NP) Ideology Constitutional Development

The National Party (NP) came to power in 1948 and strengthen the policy of apartheid through oppressive methods. Although, apartheid (Right from Land Act 1913) is most often thought of as a ideological and legislative commitment to racial separation and segregation in a system, in which whites dominate and discriminate against blacks, apartheid also involved high levels of state repression and intense economic exploitation of black South Africans.[5] Apartheid rule was not without challenge and contradictions.[6] The 1963 Constitution of republic of South Africa ignored the right to black and coloured community and faced the apartheid policies again by immoral laws. The 1983 Constitution of Tripod Parliament bolstered white rule by bringing the Indian and colored political representation as junior partners to whites. The black South Africans were completely excluded and were supposed to seek political rights in the rural bantustans and urban townships only. This Constitution was ratified in a 1983 referendum by a majority of the white South African electorate.

The referendum March 1992 on constitutional revision, de Klerk announced that South Africa's whites had closed the book on apartheid and reiterated an earlier pledge that the NP would utilize its parliamentary majority to implement decisions that called for admission of all South Africans to the political process. The NP emerged from the election of April 1994 as the second ranked party, with de Klerk as deputy president in the Mandela administration.[7]

At the Congress of the National Party in September 1996, the premier of the Western Cape, Hernus Kriel, announced that the party's policy had to be 'fair and based on what was right and not what was popular".[8] The party leader F.W. de Klerk, attending the Congress of 700 people, stated that it was clear the country was beginning to 'reap the bitter fruits of the abuse of affirmative action and insufficient financial control. The National Party, he urged, had to prove it could govern better than the ANC.[9] The party has renamed itself and is known as New National Party (NNP).

The NNP is committed to a non-racial, non-sexist, multiparty democracy that recognises the central role of the family and the community. Principles such as law and order, the rule of law, a free-enterprise economy with social responsibility, federalism and inclusive government is the foundation of party's platform. The NNP proposes a three tier government in which full legislative and executive functions and authority are conferred on Central Government and regional, local authority.

Dr. S.C. Sanam said, "A three-tier system of government takes account of the rich diversity of the population of South Africa the needs if communities in regional and local context, and the consequent need for itself determination in regional and local context."[10] A clear separation of the legislative, executive and judicial powers is a characteristic of modern democracies South separation in accepted as an essential feature of a new dispensation in South Africa. The National Party accepts the rule of law as the foundation on which such and eavours must be based.[11]

The concept of "Constitutional State", expresses the view that the constitution of a country should regulate the power of government in such a way that freedom, justice and legal certainly are guaranteed for all.[12]

The NNP has dominated in the province of Western Cape. It has given its own provincial Constitution and the constitutional court has recognized it. It embodies a spirit of common purpose, inclusiveness and co-operation through its multiparty provincial cabinet. It believes that it can became a model for the Central Government.

Human Rights and Democratic Party—Constitutional Proposals

Nature of the Constitution

1. The Democratic Party believes that to be durable and binding a new constitution for South Africa must be the expression of the will of all the people of our country. As such, it should be the product of negotiation between political leader and endorsed by the people as a whole.

2. The Democratic Party believes that the Constitution is more fundamental than the ordinary law. This is so because the constitution determines the basic rights of citizens, and the framework within which the ordinary law is made. The DP believes that this constitution must be founding document for the 'new South Africa', specifying amongst other things.

- A statement of ideals
- The relationship between the major organs of government, the power and functions of there, the eligibility of people to serve on them and method by which they are elected or appointed.
- The division, of powers, functions and responsibilities between the various branches of government and the distribution of powers, functions and responsibilities between the different levels of government;
- The rights of individuals and the obligations of government and the way in which such rights and obligations are enforced or protected and
- The mechanisms by which the constitution or parts of it are protected and/or can be amended.
- The Democratic Party believes that the constitution should be beyond the whim of transient majorities in the legislature and should only be amended by following special procedure which make the amending process much more difficult than the ordinary legislative process. The amending procedure should itself be entrenched to prevent manipulation.
- The Democratic Party believes that the people must govern, and that there is no more effective way of giving this expression than for the constitution to provide for a variety of sites of power in which the people themselves can participate in making decisions affecting them.
- Federalism in a defence against tyranny-: The Democratic party believes that an over-concentration of power in central government lead to the retention of power for its own sake, and use of power and patronage for the advantage of the party or group which is in power. South Africa's history of littered with examples of the use of the monopoly of centralized political power to

impose an oppressive philosophy on the entire country. A federal structure makes this very much more difficult and the system also provide a variety of sites of power in which more people can exercise power, making the retention of central government power relatively less important.

– The Democratic Party accepts the boundaries of country as established at the time of Union, and believes that the TBVC countries should be part of a common South Africa the mechanics of how the TBVC states return to form part of South Africa will, however, have to be negotiated with representative leadership in those countries. Within these boundaries of South Africa, various options for the delineation of federal units should be considered.

– The DP envisages 8 to 12 federal states, but the exact number of states and the delineation of boundaries could be determined by an impartial delimitation commission. However, the following criteria must be taken into account in determining the boundaries:

(a) The firm rejection of states delineated in racial or ethnic level;

(b) Community of interests of the population of an area;

(c) Economic viability and potential; and

(d) Administrative effectiveness.

Separation of Powers : The federal government will exercise those powers essentials to the national interest. All other power will be exercised by the state governments. The state governments could, for example, handle the following powers, health, local government, licensing, town planning, local taxation, nature conservation and tourism promotion, roads, education, police, prison and land settlement.

- The federal government would exercise *inter alia* the following powers; foreign relations, economic affairs, water affairs, labour, citizenship, currency, inter-state commerce, defence, borrowing on the credit of the government, emigration, foreign trade, customs and excise, national transportation and mineral and energy affairs. Certain institutions, such as a federal investigation bureau, may require management by both central and federal governments. Joint Committee of the central and state governments may be established for the purposes of liaison and cooperation.
- Financial relations between the states and Central Government. Each state shall have the power to raise its own taxes.
- The Bill of Civil Rights and the statement of Social, Economic and cultural obligations of Government.

The Bill of Civil Rights will guarantee all persons irrespective of race, ethnicity, colour, religion, gender, sexual preference or other arbitrary criteria, the following basic rights:-

(a) Equal protection of the laws.

(b) Personal liberty saw by due process of law in the ordinary courts of the land

(c) Freedom of speech and expression

(d) Freedom of movement

(e) Freedom of association

(f) Freedom of worship

(g) The rights of peaceful assembly

(h) The right to privacy of home and correspondence

(i) The right to own, acquire, occupy and dispose of property and the right to compensation in the event of expropriation

(j) The right to start and carry on any lawful trade, business, profession or occupation

(k) The guarantee of regular and free elections.

The statement of Social, Economic and cultural obligations of Government shall contain at least the following :

(a) The obligation of government to respect the national symbols and traditions of groups;

(b) The necessity for government to actively address the huge economic, social and developmental backlogs which exist.

(c) The responsibility to ensure a clean and healthy environment and to protect the natural resource of the country;

(d) The duty to apply affirmative action programmes in the public sector as long as these are needed.

Form of Central Government

The Democratic Party believes in separation of powers between the legislature, the executive and the judiciary.

The Executive—The DP proposes a executive consisting of a President and a Prime Minister together with a cabinet drawn from and accountable to Parliament. The President shall be directly elected on the basis of universal adult franchise for a period of seven years. A system run-offs will ensure that the person elected enjoys majority support.

(a) He will be commander-in-chief of the defence force and will preside over meetings of the high command of the defence force;

(b) He will appoint the Prime Minister and President of the senate, and as the advise of the Prime Minister will appoint Ministers of State;

(c) He will be available to resolute deadlocks which may occur in the cabinet;

(d) He will shape foreign policy, and will appoint ambassadors subject to confirmation by the Senate;

(e) He will negotiate treaties, and subject to approval by the Senate sign them on behalf of the government;

(f) He may declare states of National Disaster and Emergency provided that parliament shall not be dissolved during the exercise of emergency powers by the President;

(g) He may proclaim referenda and plebiscites;

(h) He may canmate criminal sentences, or grant partial or complete pardon or declare amnesties;

(i) He may confer titles and honor;

(j) He may communicate with the National Assembly and Senate by message and will annually address both Houses on the Senati of the Nation.

(k) Should the Prime Minister and the cabinet cease to enjoy the confidence of the National Assembly, the President may dissolute the National Assembly and call a general election or, alternatively, nominate some one else as Prime Minister, and call on him to form a cabinet that does enjoy the confidence of the National Assembly.

(l) The Legislature–There shall be a bicameral legislature consisting of a National Assembly and a Senate. The National Assembly and the Senati will have co-equal power except in respect of appropriation and other money bills, where the National Assembly will be able to override the objection of the Senate.

(m) The National Assembly will consist of 350 members elected on the basis of proportional representation by all adult citizens at intervals of not more than five years.

(n) The Senate, consisting of 100 members, will be elected.The election of the Senate shall take place every seven years on the same day as the election of the President.

The Judiciary

(o) There should be a single judicial system for all South Africa. The federal supreme court should be the highest Judicial body in the country and should hear appeals to this court from the various state courts.

(p) A constitutional Court should be established to interpret the Constitution the Bill of Civil Rights and the statement of social, economic and cultural obligations of government. Federal judges should be appointed from the legal profession on the advise of a judicial Appointment Commission representing the judiciary and the legal profession, and approved by the Senate. In making its recommendation, the judicial Appointments Commission representing the judiciary and the legal profession, and approved by the Senate.

The Ombudsperson

A parliamentary ombudsperson should be appointed to investigate complaints on all aged asure of power or violation of basic rights and freedoms by the executive military or police. Such officers should also be appointed in respect of the Senate legislatures. The Ombuds person should be independent, given security of tenure and adequate staff and should have investigative powers, they should be officers of the parliaments concerned.

All adult citizens, irrespective of race, religion, national origin or gender should have a vote of equal value in elections for representation of legislative institutions at all levels.

A multiparty system is essential to guarantee true democracy and the constitution should guarantee regular and free elections.

The electoral system must produce a result that ensures that the opinion and various interests of the electorate are fairly represented and must not be capable of being manipulated at the expense of minorities.

The Democratic party favours a proportional representation voting system.

National Symbols

New National symbols, must be adopted which symbolize unity and common Nationhood. Because of the potentially divisive effect of adopting national symbols which represent only sections of the community, the greatest amount of consultation and popular participation aimed at achieving the broadest consensus should precede the adoption of new symbol.

Language

The Democratic Party uphold the rights of all South African to speak their own language although a single language of record may be required. The various languages of South Africa represent are of our greatest cultural assets and should therefore, enjoy constitutional protection. In addition, languages should be promoted by means of federal and state appropriations for dictionaries, linguistic research and the arts, channelled through cultural councils.

Each federal state would, in addition to the language as record, be entitled to adopt further languages as official languages.

The right as linguistic communities to choose mother tongue education and to promote their culture, should be constitutionally protected.

Role of Inkatha Freedom Party in the Development of Human Rights in New South Africa

The National Inkatha liberation movement claims to have grown from a 'A cultural organiztion in 1920 established by King Soloman. The objective was "to presence the unity of the Zulu Nation", at a time when people's right were being undermined and their land removed. [13] The 1990 development and the IFP role related to it emphasises the establishment of a free and democratic society in a new South Africa. The IFP regards itself as upholding democratic principles and does not want a centralized state. But the party acknowledges the Constitution as the 'supreme law of the country and firmly believes in the concept of constitution.

The South African state shall comprise all the territories that formed part of South Africa as at 1910. It is envisaged that the constitution shall have jurisdiction over the whole of South Africa and that a way will be found, through negotiations to enable Transkei, Ciskei, Bophuthatswana and Venda to reaccede to the new United Republic of South Africa.

The Westminster model on which the original constitution of South Africa was based is one that is familiar to most South Africans. All South Africans have been accustomed to the idea that the Parliament at Cape Town was responsible for all the laws in the country. All legal studies, constitutional history and practice in our country have been based on that model. It is for that reason, *inter alia*, that the IFP has always preferred a single supreme legislature with power to legislate for the whole country.

At the National Convention which produced the first constitution of the South African state, the arguments in favour of a unitary as against a federal state included the idea that it was necessary to ensure that all parts of the country pursued a uniform "Native" policy. History has recorded what that meant in practice. Once more voices are being heard arguing that the merits of all-powerful centralized legislature will ensure that uniform policies are pursued throughout the country. The reasons given have nothing to do with ensuring full democratic participation for all the people.

Recent history in Africa and elsewhere has compelled the IFP to look again at the merits or otherwise of the unitary state as compared with the federal. The conclusion of the IFP is that there is much to be said on both sides. The IFP will therefore approach this issue with an open mind. The IFP has been unable to find a model of dictatorship that did not include a high degree of centralisation and desire for legislative uniformity with a minimum devolution of power. It is not the unitary or federal label that will determine the attitude to be adopted to the new constitution. The test will lie in the effectiveness of the division of powers between the central legislature and the regional or state legislatures.

The IFP constitutional proposals will be capable of adaptation either to the unitary or federal structure of government.

Fundamental Rights and Freedoms

The proposals of the IFP include detailed Bill of Rights. The text of the Bill of Rights is virtually identical to that which was included in the KwaZulu-Natal Indaba proposals for state government.

The Executive

It should be noted that in strict legal terms the Executive Government of the Republic is vested in a State President. The proposals in effect, however, envisage a division of executive power between the State President and a Prime Minister who heads a Cabinet. The powers of the State President will be carefully defined. Some powers the President will exercise in accordance with his own deliberate judgement and others will be exercised in accordance with the advice and consent of the Prime Minister. The effect will be similar to the so-called cohabitation system of the French Constitution.

The Legislature

(a) The lower House or National Assembly will be elected by universal adult suffrage by means of proportional representation. It is from the majority party or coalition in this house that a Prime Minister will be chosen to head a cabinet appointed by the said Prime Minister.

(b) The second house or Senate should represent the regions or States as well as any special interests which it is felt should be represented in the legislature.

Laws will require to be passed by majorities in both houses of Parliament and assented to by the State President to be valid.

It is proposed that the two houses of parliament should have equal powers to initiate legislation except that the budget should be initiated in the lower house or National Assembly. In other words the power to levy taxes or to make appropriations should be the preserve of the National Assembly. But in general that what is envisaged is legislative practice akin to that of the two houses of Congress in the United States constitution. It is considered that in the conditions of the modern world the idea of an upper house which has merely the negative powers of delay, review and veto is not good constitutional practice. The upper house should in fact be fully functioning house. This would compel a system of constructive co-operation between the two houses of Parliament.

It is already apparent that difficulties may be experienced in negotiations over the constitution of the Senate which is designed to reflect substantially interests which may not always coincide with the wishes of the lower house. But this should not be assumed. The democratically elected Senate composed largely of regional or state representatives could very well also reflect the majority party or coalition in the National Assembly.

State Government

A great deal of attention was devoted to the subject in the KwaZulu-Natal Indaba and the conclusions thereof were by and large welcomed by the IFP as a good starting point. Following up on the KwaZulu-Natal Indaba proposals the IFP proposes that the existing provinces, national states and (if they re-accede to the RSA) the independent states should be replaced by the creation of State governments based on more logical economic, territorial, cultural and linguistic factors. A special state boundaries commission should be appointed immediately to consult the entire population and produce a report on State boundaries.

Each state shall have a State legislature elected on the basis of proportional representation. The powers of the States should be clearly set out in the constitution and such powers should be entrenched. The States shall have an executive headed by a State Premier and a Governor representing the central government and the State President. It should be provided that the States will have sole right to legislate on matters within their competence. It should be provided that the central legislature shall only legislate on matters within the constitutional competence of the States at the request of the State legislature or legislatures.

An apparent novelty provided for in the KwaZulu-Natal proposals was that the cabinet appointed by the Premier should reflect all the parties represented in the legislature. It was assumed that the parties concerned would tend to represent various cultural communities or the South African community as a whole. This would obviously depend on the voting patterns revealed in any state election. But the idea was to modify or eliminate the idea of "winner takes all" at the state level. The tendency away from partisanship at state or local levels is one which could encourage reconciliation and co-operation and ensure full participation by all at State and Local levels.

The Judiciary

It is proposed to appoint judges for a new judiciary. It is suggested that the constitution provide for a judicial service commission to, in effect, make recommendations to the State President for appointments to the judiciary in place of the present system. The judicial service commission under the Chairmanship of the Chief Justice shall also supervise all lower courts and appoint regional and local magistrates. The standard provisions to ensure the independence of the judiciary should be incorporated in the constitution to determine the validity of laws passed by the central legislature, the state legislatures and local authorities as well as the right to interpret laws.

This will be a departure from the present position in which the validity of parliamentary legislation cannot be questioned by the judiciary. Also the Bill of Rights shall be justiciable and thus form part of the jurisdiction of the Supreme Court.

Civil Service Commission

It is proposed that a Civil Service Commission should be set up as part of the constitution. The Civil Service Commission shall be charged with the recruitment and supervision of civil servants in accordance with Public Service Acts and with General Orders issued by the Prime Minister. It shall be the task of the Civil Service Commission, *inter alia,* to ensure that the civil service is representative of all population groups in the country in addition to its normal duties with regard to preservation of standards and merit. Special provisions shall be required initially to upgrade Blacks in the civil service taken as a whole. Such measures should include attractive compensation to encourage early retirement in order to make way for citizens hitherto excluded from the upper rungs of the public service. These provisions should be included in the constitutional powers of the Civil Service Commission.

The Disciplined Forces

The IFP is in favour of impartial, professional services owing allegiance to the constitution only. In accordance with the usual provisions in most constitutions the armed services should be the responsibility of the State President assisted by the State Security Council. But the national police should be the responsibility of the Prime Minister. Provision should be made for State and Local police operating under the jurisdiction of the State Government.

Traditional Government

The IFP is in favour of provisions that provide for recognition and powers of traditional rulers and authorities as well as courts. The present position in which these authorities are the plaything of government of the day, and numerous contradictory legislative measures must be corrected with the adoption of suitable constitutional provisions. Any participatory democracy in our country will require proper attention to be paid to this aspect. The linking of traditional authorities with economic development could ensure that progress in the country reaches down to village level thus improving the quality of life of all the people in town and country alike.

Transitional Provisions and Savings

The IFP considers that the constitutional negotiations should not be viewed as a single one-off event in which the perfect constitution will be produced at one full swoop. A situation may arise in which very substantial agreement is reached with one or two aspects that cannot be agreed. Instead of delaying implementation of democratic constitution the country may well have to settle for a flawed constitution which does not in all its aspects comply with full democracy. If, for example, special provisions have to be adopted to allay the fears of minorities these should be clearly specified and possibly given limited validity for a period of five or ten years. This would be preferable to negating the entire democratic process as a result of an all-or-nothing approach. But in general the IFP considers that the principles of democracies are fairly well known, tried and tested. These principles should not be departed from unduly by the introduction of features that are so novel and imaginative as to cast doubt on the credibility and integrity of the new constitution as an instrument of democracy and freedom. The kernel of the new democracy in South Africa is the unambiguous and clearly perceived emancipation of formerly oppressed peoples. In order to command widespread allegiance and respect the new democratic non-racial constitution must clearly reflect the freedom of the people of South Africa.

Draft Constitution for the Republic of South Africa

(i) TITLE: THE REPUBLIC OF SOUTH AFRICA CONSTITUTION ACT.

(ii) Date of Commencement. The date of commencement of the constitution shall be fixed by the State President by proclamation.

(iii) The Preamble

(iv) Fundamental Rights and Freedoms

All persons in the Republic of South Africa shall be entitled to the following fundamental human rights and freedoms.

Human dignity and equality before the law

1. (1) All human beings are born free and equal in dignity and rights.

(2) Everyone is equal before the law, and shall be entitled to equal protection of the law without distinction on the basis of race, sex, colour, language, region, nationality, ethnic or social origin, property, birth, political or other opinion or economic or other status.

Right to life

2. (1) Everyone's right to life shall be protected by law, and no one may be deprived of his life intentionally save in the execution of a sentence of a competent court following his conviction of a crime for which this penalty is provided by law.

(2) Deprivation of life shall not constitute a contravention of this article when it results from the use of such force as is absolutely necessary and justiciable in the circumstances –

(i) in defence of any person against unlawful violence;

(ii) to effect a lawful arrest in order to prevent the escape of a person.

(iii) in action lawfully taken for the purpose of quelling a riot or insurrection.

Punishment

3. No one shall be subjected to torture or to inhuman or degrading treatment or punishment.

Right to liberty

4. (1) No one shall be held in slavery or servitude.

(2) No one shall be required to perform forced or compulsory labour provided that this does not include –

(a) any normal work required to be done in the ordinary course of detention under the provisions of sub-section (3) hereunder or during conditional release from such detention;

(b) any service of a military character in terms of a law requiring citizens to undergo military training;

(c) any service exacted in case of emergency or calamity threatening the existence or well-being of the Republic;

(d) any work or service which forms part of normal civic obligations imposed by law.

(3) Everyone has the right to liberty and security of person and no one shall be deprived of his liberty save in the following cases and in accordance with a procedure prescribed by law which does not deny his basic rights to physical and mental health and integrity -

(a) the lawful detention of a person after conviction by a competent court;

(b) the lawful arrest and detention of a person for non-compliance with the lawful order of a court;

(c) the lawful arrest or detention of a person effected for the purpose of bringing him before a competent legal authority on reasonable grounds of having committed an offence or when it is reasonably considered necessary to prevent his committing an offence or fleeing after having done so;

(d) the lawful detention of a person for the prevention of the spreading of infectious diseases, of a person of unsound mind, an alcoholic or a drug addict;

(e) the lawful arrest or detention of a person to prevent his effecting an unauthorised entry into the Republic or of a person against whom action is being taken with a view to deportation or extradition.

(4) Everyone who is arrested shall be informed promptly, in a language which he understands of the reasons for his arrest and of any charge against him.

(5) Everyone arrested or detained in accordance with the provisions of subsection (3)(c) shall be brought promptly before a judge or before any other officer authorised by law to exercise judicial power and shall be entitled to trial within a reasonable time or to release pending trial, subject to such lawful conditions as may be imposed to guarantee appearance at the trial.

(6) In the determination of his civil rights and obligations or of any criminal charge against him, every one shall be entitled to a fair and public hearing within a reasonable time by an independent and impartial court established by law; judgment shall be pronounced publicly but the press and public may be excluded from all or part of the proceedings in the interests of morals, public order or national security in a democratic society, where the interests of ju veniles or the protection of the private life of parties so require, or to the extent strictly necessary in the opinion of the court in special circumstances where the publicity would prejudice the interests of justice.

(7) Everyone charged with a criminal offence shall be presumed innocent until proved guilty according to law.

(8) Everyone charged with a criminal offence shall have the right

(a) to be informed promptly, in a language of his choice which he understands and in detail, of the nature and cause of the accusation against him.

(b) To have adequate time and facilities for the preparation of his defence.

(c) To defend himself in person or through legal assistance of his own choosing or if he does not have sufficient means to pay for legal assistance to be given it at no cost to himself when the interests of justice so require.

(d) To examine or have examined witnesses against him and to obtain the attendance and examination of witnesses on his behalf under the same conditions as witnesses testifying against him.

(e) To have free assistance of an interpreter if he cannot understand or speak the language used in court or if he so requests.

(9) Everyone who is deprived of his liberty by arrest or detention shall be informed promptly in a language of his choice which he understands and in detail the reasons for his arrest and detention, and shall be entitled to take proceedings by which the lawfulness of his detention is decided speedily by a court, and be released if the detention is not lawful: Provided that if he has not sufficient means to pay for legal assistance, he will be given at no cost to himself such assistance as he requires.

(10) Everyone who has been the victim of unlawful arrest or detention shall have an enforceable right to compensation.

(11) No one who is tried for a criminal offence shall be compelled to give evidence at the trial nor should any adverse inference be drawn from his silence at such trial.

(12) No one who shows that he has been tried by a competent court for a criminal offence and either convicted or acquitted shall again be tried for that offence or for any other criminal offence of which he could have been convicted at the trial for the offence, save upon order of a Superior Court in the course of appeal or review proceedings relating to his conviction or acquittal.

(13) No one shall be found guilty of any penal offence on account of any act or omission which did not constitute a penal offence at the time when it was committed.

(14) No act or omission shall constitute an offence unless such offence is specifically defined and has a penalty attached to it by a law published in the customary manner.

Rights to Administrative or Natural Justice

5. (1) All administrative tribunals, public authorities and officials shall follow the rules of natural justice or fundamental fairness in coming to their decisions and they shall, unless inappropriate, be required to furnish reasons for such decisions.

(2) Delegated legislation shall be drafted with a reasonable allowance for public comment and participation.

(3) Everyone who has suffered damage as a result of unlawful action by public authority shall have an enforceable right to compensation.

Right to privacy and protection of the family

6. (1) No one shall be subjected to arbitrary interference with his privacy, family, home or communications, nor to attacks upon his honour and reputation.

Right to Property

7. (1) Everyone has the right to lawfully own and occupy property anywhere in the Republic.

(2) No one shall be deprived of his property without due process of law, and expropriation by public authorities may only be authorities in terms of a law if it is for the public benefit and if equitable and fair compensation is promptly paid.

(3) Land and natural resources shall not be expropriated except for the common good and in accordance with laws providing for equitable compensation.

Ethnic, religious, linguistic, cultural and educational rights

8. (1) A person belonging to an ethnic, religious or linguistic group shall not be denied the right to enjoy his own culture, to profess and practise his own religion or to use his own language.

(2) Everyone shall have the right freely to participate in the cultural life of the Republic to enjoy the arts, to share in scientific advancement and benefits, and to free and full development of his personality.

(3) In all proceedings inVolving customary law followed by persons in the Republic such law may be applied except in as far as the courts find that it has fallen into disuse or is contrary to the principles of natural justice and morality,

(4) Every person shall have the same right to public ducation in an institution that will cater for his interests and abilities, aptitudes and interests and the Republic or other authorities in the Republic shall make provision for this right without discrimination: Provided that notwithstanding the provisions of section 1 (12), it may,be in providing facilities, distinguish between persons on grounds of language or sex.

Freedom of Movement

9. Everyone shall have the right to freedom of movement within the Republic or to travel abroad.

Freedom of Thought, Conscience and Religion

10. (1) Everyone shall be entitled to freedom of thought, conscience and religion and to change his religion or belief, to manifest his religion or belief in worship, teaching, practice and observance, whether alone or in community with others in public or in private.

(2) No one shall be compelled against his religious convictions to render military service inVolving the use of arms but shall be required to render national service as provided by law in lieu thereof.

Freedom of Expression and Opinion

11. (1) Everyone shall be entitled to freedom of opinion and expression, which includes the freedom to hold opinions

without interference and to seek and impart information and ideas.

(2) An advocacy of national, racial or religious hatred and aggression between groups and individuals that constitutes incitement to discrimination, hostility, violence or political animosity is prohibited and a law may be passed providing penalties for breach of this provision.

Freedom of Association

12. (1) Everyone shall be entitled to freedom of peaceful assembly and to freedom of association with others, including the right to form and to join trade unions for the protection of his interests, and no one may be compelled to belong to an association.

(2) Everyone shall be free to form or to join political parties in order to participate in periodic and free elections, which shall be held by secret ballot or by equivalent free voting procedures.

Freedom of Work and Freedom of Contract

13. (1) Everyone shall be entitled to equal work opportunities and to free choice of employment.

(2) Everyone with legal capacity shall have freedom to contract and to conclude agreements with others in the Voluntary exercise of his rights and freedoms and generally for the promotion of his interests.

Restrictions on Rights and Freedoms

14. (1) The rights and freedoms recognised under the provisions of the Bill of Rights may be restricted by law for reasons which are necessary in a free and democratic society in the interests of public safety for the prevention of disorder or crime, for the protection of health and morals, for the protection of the rights, freedoms and reputation

of others, and for main-taining the authority and impartiality of the judiciary and for the social, moral and economic well-being of all the inhabitants of the Republic.

(2) Everyone's exercise of his right and freedoms shall be subject to such limitations as are legally determined for the purpose of securing due recognition and respect for the rights and freedoms of others, and groups which by reason of their aims and the behaviour of their adherents, seek to impair or abolish the free democratic order or to endanger the security of the Republic are prohibited.

(3) A fundamental right and freedom protected in this Bill of Rights may not be abolished or in its essence be encroached upon by any law of the Republic.

Enforcement of Rights and Freedoms

15. (1) The rights and freedoms protected in the Bill of Rights are binding on the Parliament, the executive, the judiciary and all government and State institutions in the Republic and any person may forthwith apply to the Supreme Court or to other competent authorities provided for in this Constitution by appropriate proceedings or by Petition to enforce these rights and freedoms.

(2) The Supreme Court shall have jurisdiction and power to make all such orders as may be necessary and appropriate to secure to the applicant the enjoyment of any rights and freedoms conferred by the provisions of this Bill of Rights: Provided that if at the commencement of this Constitution there are laws in existence in the Republic which are inconsistent with this Bill of Rights, such laws may, after the lapse of one year after the commencement of this Constitution and on application to the Supreme Court be declared void to the extent of such inconsistency.

The Executive

A. The State President

1. The Executive government of the Republic of South Africa shall vest in "the State President who shall be Head of State and Commander-in-Chief of the armed forces.

2. The executive powers of the State President shall include those powers exercised by the State President -

   (a) Directly in accordance with his own deliberate judgement.

   (b) In accordance with the advice and consent of the Prime Minister.

   (c) After consultation with designated persons, authorities or institutions although not bound to follow advice emanating from such consultation.

   (d) In terms of this Constitution or any law.

3. Without in any way limiting their generality the powers vested in the State President shall include, *inter alia*, the

   (i) Convocation, prorogation, recall or dissolution of Parliament.

   (ii) Appointment of the Prime Minister in terms of the constitution

   (iii) Appointment of Cabinet Ministers and other Ministers of State

   (iv) Appointment of the Chief Justice and other judges of the Supreme Court

   (v) Appointment of State Governors

   (vi) Appointment and accredition of Ambassadors an other envoys of the State

   (vii) Appointment of Senior Commanders and Officers of the armed forces

(viii) Appointment of specific senior public servants

(ix) Declaration of State of Emergency or Martial law

(x) State emblems, flags and privileges

(xi) State Honours and Decorations

(xii) Exercise of the Prerogative of Mercy and Pardon of persons convicted of any offence

(xiii) Residual powers in respect of any matter not specifically provided for in any law

4. There shall be a Council of State which shall consist of the Prime Minister and two other Ministers designated by him and other members appointed by the State President without restriction as to number.

5. There shall be a State Security Council consisting of such members of the armed forces and security services as shall be appointed by the State President together with the Prime Minister and Minister of Defence.

6. There shall be an Executive Council which shall consist of the Prime Minister and members of the Cabinet presided over by the State President.

7. At least once a year there shall be a meeting of the State Governors which shall be presided over by the State President.

8. There shall be an Office of the State President whose accommodation, officers and staff throughout the coun try shall be as determined by the State President.

B. The Prime Minister

9. The State President shall appoint the Prime Minister who shall be head of the Central Government and administration of the Republic. The State President shall appoint as Prime Minister the person who appears to enjoy the confidence of the majority of members of the National Assembly or Lower House of Parliament.

The State President acting in accordance with the advice and consent of the Prime Minister, shall appoint such Cabinet Ministers outside the Cabinet, Deputy Ministers as shall be designated by the Prime Minister to head Ministries or Departments of Government. There shall be a Cabinet which shall consist of such Ministers as are designated by the Prime Minister. The meetings of the Cabinet shall be presided over by the Prime Minister.

There shall be an office of the Prime Minister and other Ministers and Departments which shall be staffed and accommodated as determined by the Prime Minister or by laws relating to the Public Service.

The Legislature

Laws providing for the peace order and good government of the Republic shall be enacted by Parliament which shall consist of the National Assembly, (or Lower House), the Senate (or Upper House) and the State President acting together.

In order to be valid laws shall require to be passed by a majority in both Houses of Parliament and to be assented to by the State President.

The two Houses of Parliament shall have equal powers to initiate legislation except that the power to raise revenue and make appropriations shall be reserved to the National Assembly. With respect to the annual budget the Senate shall have the right only to delay passage.

(a) The National Assembly : The National Assembly shall consist of approximately 400 members elected by all citizens of the Republic on a common roll based on universal adult suffrage. The system of election shall be by proportional representation.

(b) The Senate : The Senate shall consist of approximately 180 members representing the States or regions and any special interest which it is thought should be part of the legislative process. Each House of Parliament shall determine its own procedure.

Proceedings of the National Assembly shall be presided over by the Speaker of the House. Proceedings of the Senate shall be presided over by the President of the Senate.

State Government

The Republic shall be divided into States whose boundaries shall be determined on logical economic, territorial cultural and other relevant factors. Each state shall have a State Legislature elected by the registered voters of that State. There shall be a State Executive, headed by the State Premier and a State Governor representing the Central Government and the State President in the State concerned.

The powers of the States shall be as set out clearly in the constitution. Such powers shall be exercised exclusively by the States unless a State, a number of States or all the States request that the Central legislature should legislate on a subject. The Central legislature shall not have power to legislate on matters which the constitution reserves for the States. Provision for the re-accession of the independent states or any other state should be made in the constitution.

The Judiciary

There shall be a Supreme Court in each state and the Appellate Division which shall be the highest court in the land. The judiciary shall be headed by the Chief Justice of South Africa who shall be appointed by the State President in consultation with the Prime Minister from among Members of the judiciary. The Chief Justice shall preside over the Judicial Service Commission which shall make recommendations on judicial appointments to the State President.

The Public Service

There shall be a Civil Service Commission whose members shall be appointed by the State President, acting on the advice and consent of the Prime Minister. It shall be duty of the Civil Service

Commission to make appointments, promote and otherwise supervise the civil service in accordance with the Public Service Acts, General Orders and other relevant legislation.

It shall be the duty of the Civil Service Commission to reorganise the civil service so that it more fairly reflects the composition of the South African population on the basis of merit. The Civil Service Commission shall also introduce measures to upgrade citizens who were previously denied access to the higher rungs of the Civil Service.

Traditional Government

The constitution shall make specific provisions regarding the recognition and status of traditional authorities and shall provide for the establishment of a House of Chiefs consisting of traditional and modern leaders. The constitution should provide for general principles to guide legislation for the creation of the House of Chiefs, its status and role in the South African polity.

Defence and Security

The constitution shall make provision for the establishment of the armed forces and security services of the Republic. It shall be provided that the army, police, prison and security forces generally shall be truly non-racial and professional owing allegiance to the constitution only. The constitution shall set out the principles that should guide the separate legislation setting up the defence establishment, the police, prison and security services.

Transitional Arrangements and Service Entrenched Clauses

The constitution shall set out the clauses of the constitution that are entrenched and therefore require special provisions for their amendment.

Amendments of the Constitution

The constitution itself shall be entrenched as a whole, so that special provisions for amending entrenched clauses shall naturally also apply to amendments of the constitution itself.

Repeal of laws and other consequential provisions

The Cost of the New Constitution

Over the years there has been the suggestion that the government of South Africa as a whole is encumbered by a huge bureaucracy and unnecessary duplication. It has also been suggested that the creation of number of State Legislatures and governments in place of the current provinces and homeland governments will be expensive or similarly expensive.

To meet these objections it seems necessary to do an actual cost exercise to determine the cost of a new constitution including State President, Office of the State President, Prime Minister, Office of the Prime Minister, Cabinet, Senate, National Assembly, State Government including Governor, Premier and Legislature.

The number of States will obviously be crucial. At present we have a Tri-cameral Parliament and fourteen other governments if one includes the provinces, independent homelands and self-governing homeland governments. The NP proposals envisages nine regional governments. It is understood that the ANC is ready to propose fourteen regional governments. It may be that nine are required together with Metropolitan Johannesburg as a tenth State on its own. The question of where the capital will be is also likely to be a strong subject for negotiation review, and the guarantee of the political rights of all groups. Equality before the law, equality of opportunity and equality of benefit from the institute of the state, is provided and incorporated in the Fundamental Right for every individual. The administration of law and justice should be carried out in a fair and impartial way in the interest of the individual. Emergence has the right to lawfully own and occupy property anywhere in the republic. Everyone's right to life shall be protected/ by law's in defence of any person against unlawful violences.

The Democratic Party and Human Rights

The Democratic Party was formed April 8, 1989 when the former Progressive Federal Party independent Party and National

Democratic Movement merged. Under the combined leadership of Zach de Bur, Denes Worrall, Malan, the DP was 36 seats in Parliament in the general elections of September 1999.

However, the history of the Democratic Party goes back to 1959 when a number of liberal member of the United Party broke away to form the Progressive Party. The cause of the split was the United Party's inability to find a clear-cut alternative to the National Party's apartheid policy. The Progressive Party took its stand on constitutional reform, calling for an entrenched constitution incorporating a Bill of Rights, for an independent judiciary and for a federal Constitution in which the powers of the provinces would be constitutionally protected.

The April 1994 general elections were the liberation elections, the first in which all South African vote together. The Democratic Party was winning only 1.7 per cent of the vote on the national level, having only 10 members of Parliments. Underf the leadership of Tony Leon, the Democratic Party's began a new fight, the fight for the protection of human rights and the extension of federalism and free enterprise in South Africa.

1. BASIC POINTS OF DEPARTURE

1.1 The Nature of the Constitution

The Democratic Party believes that to be durable and binding, a new constitution for South Africa must be the expression of the will of all the people of our country. As such, it should be the product of negotiation between political leaders, and endorsed by the people as a whole. Because the new constitution will represent a fundamental break with the past, the DP believes that this constitution must be the founding document for the "new South Africa", specifying, amongst other things.

- A statement (preamble) of ideals;
- The relationship between the major organs of government, the powers and functions of these, the

eligibility of people to serve on them and the method by which they are elected or appointed;

- The division of powers, functions and responsibilities between the various branches of government and the distribution of powers, functions and responsibilities between the different levels of government;
- The rights of individuals and the obligations of government, and the way in which such rights and obligations are enforced or protected
- The mechanisms by which the constitution or parts of it are protected and/or can be amended.

1.2 The DP believes that the constitution is superior to the ordinary law

The Democratic Party believes that the constitution is more fundamental than the ordinary law. This is so because the constitution determines the basic rights of citizens, and the framework within which the ordinary law is made. This implies that the constitution and constitutional laws must be less easily amended than the ordinary law.

1.3 The DP believes in the supremacy of the constitution

Because the constitution is more fundamental than the ordinary law, the courts (or some specialized branch of the courts) must be able to render null and void legislative provisions or executive acts which violate the rights of individuals, or the basic principles contained in the constitution.

1.4 The DP believes that the constitution should be rigid

The Democratic Party believes that the constitution should be beyond the whim of transient majorities in the legislature and should only be amended by following special procedures which make the amending process much more difficult than the ordinary legislative process. The amending procedure should itself be entrenched to prevent manipulation. Such a process may involve special majorities, referenda, endorsement by state legislatures or other means. The constitution may provide for different processes of amendment in respect of different aspects of the constitution, but the method of amendment should itself be protected by special procedures, and subject to judicial review.

1.5 The DP believes in the maximum devolution of power

The Democratic Party believes that the people must govern, and that there is no more effective way of giving this expression than for the constitution to provide for a variety of sites of power in which the people themselves can participate in making decisions affecting them.

2. FEDERALISM

Federalism will distribute power

By providing a variety of different sites of power, federalism enables more people to take part in the process of government. It also brings government closer to the people. This promotes accountability of political office-bearers to their constituents, and promotes the establishment of a democratic culture.

Federalism is a defence against tyranny

The Democratic Party believes that an over-concentration of power in central government leads to the retention of power for its own sake, and the use of power and patronage for the advantage of the party or group which is in power. South Africa's history is littered with examples of the use of the monopoly of centralized political power to impose an oppressive philosophy on the entire country. A federal structure makes this very much more difficult, and the system also provides a variety of sites of power in which more people can exercise power, making the retention of central government power relatively less important.

Federalism accommodates pluralism

The Democratic Party accepts the cultural, linguistic, geographic and political pluralism of South Africa. This diversity is a national asset which needs to be developed in a spirit of mutual respect, tolerance and conciliation. Federalism helps to cater for this diversity by multiplying the sites of power.

Moreover, by multiplying sites of power and competition, new and transcending alliances based on regional or common interests can be forged, which can lead to the resolution of problems and issues at a localized level. This will certainly make the resolution of seemingly intractable problems far easier..

How federalism will be established

Federal constitutions occur in two ways.

(a) when formerly sovereign polities surrender part of this sovereignty to supranational legislative, executive and judicial authorities.

(b) when the powers hitherto exercised on central government level are restricted and are consciously and deliberately deVolved to regional political authorities.

In South Africa's case, the second route is more likely to be followed.

It is essential, however, that in this process the equal rights, powers and responsibilities of such regional political authorities are written into and entrenched in the constitution. It is a central tenet of DP policy that the central parliament will enjoy coordinate sovereignty with the state parliaments. It is also essential that the constitution guarantees equitable access by regional political authorities to the resources of the nation as a whole; otherwise any rights, powers and responsibilities of such authorities will be meaningless.

The Boundaries of the federation

The Democratic Party accepts the boundaries of the country as established at the time of Union, and believes that the TBVC countries should be part of a common South Africa. The mechanics of how the TBVC states return to form part of South Africa will, however, have to be negotiated with representative leadership in those countries. Within these boundaries of South Africa, various options for the delineation of federal units should be considered.

One option would be to create federal units of roughly equal population, and/or geographic size, and/or wealth and power. Another option would be to create federal states around the present economic development regions. A third alternative would be for federal boundaries to be drawn on a metropole- periphery basis.

The DP envisages 8 to 12 federal states, but the exact number of states and the delimitation of boundaries could be determined by an impartial delimitation commission. However, the following criteria must be taken into account in determining the boundaries:

- the firm rejection of states delineated on racial or ethnic lines;
- Community of interests of the population of an area;
- Economic viability and potential; and
- Administrative effectiveness.

The Powers of the Central Government and the Federal States

In the process of drawing up a new constitution, the powers exercised by the federal government and those exercised by the states will have to be specifically defined and entrenched. The federal government will exercise those powers essential to the national interest. All other powers will be exercised by the state governments. The state governments could, for example, handle the following powers: health, local government; licensing, town planning, local taxation, nature conservation and tourism promotion, roads, education, police, prisons, and land settlement.

The federal government would exercise *inter alia* the following powers: foreign relations, economic affairs, water affairs, labour, citizenship, currency, inter-state commerce, defence, borrowing on the credit of the government, emigration, foreign trade, customs and excise, national transportation and mineral and energy affairs. Certain institutions, such as a Federal Investigation Bureau, may require management by both central and federal governments. Joint committees of the central and state governments may be established for the purposes of liaison and cooperation.

The Structure of State and Local Governments

The structure of state government should be laid down and protected in the constitution. Local governments should as far as practical be established on the same basis as first and second tier structures. The question of majorities, entrenched sections and vetoes, where applicable, should be contained in the constitutions of all levels of government. Very importantly, the Bill of Rights must be enforceable at all levels of government and administration.

Financial relations between the States and Central Government

Each state shall have the power to raise its own taxes.

A fiscal commission must be established to investigate the reasonable cost to each federal state and to the central federal government of administering the various areas of responsibility assigned to each state in such a way as to ensure equal quality of services as between the various states. Further, a Federal Finance Council comprising representatives of the federal and state governments and expert bureaucrats should be established. It would examine state budgets and the federal budget to determine the amount of revenue and loan funds which each state could claim from the Federal Treasury. There are many other possible methods of ensuring that each state receives prorata its rightful share of financial resources but whatever mechanism is adopted should be trenched in the constitution.

3. Central Government

Separation of powers

Subject to the executive being accountable to parliament for its administration, there should be the maximum amount of separation of powers between the legislature, the executive and the judiciary.

The Executive

The DP proposes a (dual) executive consisting of a President and a Prime Minister together with a Cabinet drawn from and accountable to Parliament. The President shall be directly elected on the basis of universal adult franchise for a period of seven years. A system of run-offs will ensure that the person elected enjoys majority support. The President, in addition to being Head of State, will have defined powers, as follows :

(a) he will be commander-in-chief of the defence force and will preside over meetings of the high command of the defence force;

(b) he will appoint the Prime Minister and President of the Senate, and, on the advice of the Prime Minister, will appoint Ministers of State;

(c) he will be available to resolve deadlocks which may occur in the Cabinet;

(d) he will shape foreign policy, and will appoint ambassadors subject to confirmation by the Senate;

(e) he will negotiate treaties, and subject to approval by the Senate; sign them on behalf of the government;

(f) he may declare States of National Disaster and Emergency provided that Parliament shall not be dissolved during the exercise of emergency powers by the President;

(g) he may proclaim referenda and plebiscites;

(h) he may commute criminal sentences, or grant partial or complete pardon, or declare amnesties;

(i) he may confer titles and honours;

(j) he may communicate with the National Assembly and Senate by message and will annually address both Houses on the State of the Nation.

The President will appoint a member of the National Assembly as Prime Minister who is capable of forming a Cabinet which enjoys the support of the National Assembly. The Cabinet will be constituted on a proportional basis from representatives of political parties enjoying 10 per cent or more support in the National Assembly. The right to allocate portfolios within the Cabinet shall be vested in the Prime Minister. Should the Prime Minister and the Cabinet cease to enjoy the confidence of the National Assembly, the President may dissolve the National Assembly and call a general election or, alternatively, nominate someone else as Prime Minister, and call on him to form a Cabinet that does enjoy the confidence of the National Assembly.

The Legislature

There shall be a bicameral legislature consisting of a National Assembly and a Senate. The National Assembly and the Senate will have co-equal powers except in respect of appropriation and other money bills, where the National Assembly will be able to override the objection of the Senate. The National Assembly will consist of 350 members elected on the basis of proportional representation by all adult citizens at intervals of not more than five years.

The Senate, consisting of 100 members, will be elected as follows :

(a) 66 members will be directly elected by universal franchise on the basis that each state is entitled to an equal number of senators;

(b) 33 members will be indirectly elected by all municipal councillors within a particular state, sitting together as an electoral college, on the basis of proportional representation; and

(c) The President of the Senate, who will be appointed by the President.

The election of the Senate shall take place every seven years on the same day as the election of the President. In addition to its legislative functions, the Senate will also have special powers to approve treaties and to approve senior appointments to the public service and diplomatic corps recommended by the President. In cases of legislative deadlock between the National Assembly and the Senate, a standing committee shall be appointed consisting of equal numbers of members of each House to resolve the deadlock. There shall be a system of inter-house standing committees, with the following specific powers and operating as follows :

(a) the members of each house will vote separately except in the case of a standing committee set up to resolve a deadlock between the Houses, where voting will take place jointly;

(b) the standing committee will be empowered to introduce legislation to Parliament;

(c) there shall be one standing committee established to oversee the activities of the security forces, and one to oversee "clandestine operations" by the intelligence services;

(d) there will be one standing committee for each Department of State, which will scrutinize each budget vote before submission to Parliament and which will have the power to summon the Minister, the Chief Accounting Officer and any other official to account for money expended during the previous financial year, and intended expenditure during the forthcoming financial year.

The Judiciary

There should be a single judicial system for all South Africa. The Federal Supreme Court should be the highest judicial body in the country and should hear appeals to this court from the various state courts. A Constitutional Court should be established to interpret the constitution, the Bill of Civil Rights and the Statement of Social, Economic and Cultural Obligations of Government. Federal Judges should be appointed from the legal profession on the advice of a Judicial Appointments Commission representing the judiciary and the legal profession, and approved by the Senate. In making its recommendations, the Judicial Appointments Commission should consider not only demonstrable competence, but also the need for the Bench adequately to reflect the broad population of South Africa.

Administrative appointments

An efficient and accountable civil service is an essential adjunct to achieving a functional democracy in our country. For regrettable historical reasons, the public service does not remotely reflect the public it serves and this has tended to undermine public confidence in the administration of South Africa. The Democratic Party believes in equal opportunity in government service for all qualified applicants and employees and in the prohibition of discrimination in such employment on the basis of race, colour, ethnicity, gender or creed. This notwithstanding and in order to redress the imbalances of the past, there should be continuing affirmative action programmes in each government department. These programmes should govern every aspect of personnel practice in respect of employment, development, advancement and treatment of all employees. Key senior appointments, as defined, should be made by the Prime Minister acting on the advice of an independent Senior Appointments Commission, and these appointments should be endorsed by the Senate. Each federal state would likewise have a civil service charged with the administration of functions under state control.

The Ombudsperson

A parliamentary ombudsperson should be appointed to investigate complaints on alleged abuse of power or violation of basic rights and freedoms by the executive, military or police. Such officers should also be appointed in respect of the state legislatures. The ombudspersons should be independent, given security of tenure and adequate staff, and should have investigative powers. They should be officers of the parliaments concerned.

3.6.3 The Auditors-General should be given the same powers, and report in the same way.

4. THE ELECTORAL SYSTEM

Universal suffrage

All adult citizens, irrespective of race, religion, national origin or gender should have a vote of equal value in elections for representatives of legislative institutions at all levels.

Regular and free elections

A multi-party system is essential to guarantee true democracy and the constitution should guarantee regular and free elections. Such guarantees should include the maximum period between elections, the right of individuals to form and support political parties of their choice, a secret ballot and protection against harassment or intimidation of candidates and voters.

Representivity

The electoral system must produce a result that ensures that the opinion and various interests of the electorate are fairly represented, and must not be capable of being manipulated at the expense of minorities.

Proportional representation

The Democratic Party favours a proportional representation voting system. There are a variety of different proportional voting systems applicable in different parts of the world. The one which is selected for South Africa will have to be fair, enjoy legitimacy, be workable and be easily understandable even to illiterate voters.

5. The Bill of Civil Rights and the Statement of Social, Economic and Cultural Obligations of Government

The Constitution should contain a Bill of Civil Rights and a Statement of Social, Economic and Cultural Obligations of Government. The Bill of Civil Rights will guarantee all persons irrespective of race, ethnicity, colour, religion, gender, sexual preference or other arbitrary criteria, the following basic rights

(a) Equal protection of the laws

(b) Personal liberty save by due process of law in the ordinary courts of the land

(c) Freedom of speech and expression

(d) Freedom of movement

(e) Freedom of association

(f) Freedom of worship

(g) The right of peaceful assembly

(h) The right to privacy of home and correspondence

(i) The right to own, acquire, occupy and dispose of property, and the right to compensation in the event of expropriation

(j) The right to start and carry on any lawful trade, business, profession or occupation

(k) The guarantee of regular and free elections

These rights should be fully justifiable either by the constitutional court or the ordinary courts. The Statement of Social, Economic and Cultural Obligations of Government shall contain at least the following :

(a) The obligation of government to respect the national symbols and traditions of groups;

(b) The necessity for government to actively address the huge economic, social and developmental backlogs which exist;

(c) The responsibility to ensure a clean and healthy environment, and to protect the natural resources of the country;

(d) The duty to apply affirmative action programmes in the public sector as long as these are needed.

6. NATIONAL SYMBOLS

New national symbols must be adopted which symbolize unity and common nationhood. Because of the potentially divisive effect of adopting national symbols which represent only sections of the community, the greatest amount of consultation and popular participation aimed at achieving the broadest consensus should precede the adoption of new symbols. In the interim, the Democratic Party favours an incremental approach, inVolving the combining of symbols until such time as new symbols are agreed to. In particular Nkosi Sikelel Afrika and Die Stem ought to be played at all official occasions until a single national anthem is decided upon.

7. LANGUAGE

The Democratic Party upholds the right of all South Africans to speak their own language although a single language of record may be required. The various languages of South Africa represent one of our greatest cultural assets and should, therefore, enjoy constitutional protection. In addition, languages should be promoted by means of federal and state appropriations for dictionaries, linguistic research and the arts, channelled through cultural councils. Each federal state would, in addition to the language of record, be entitled to adopt further languages as official languages. The right of linguistic communities to choose mother-tongue education, and to promote their culture, should be constitutionally protected.

(a) South Africa would be divided into 100 constituencies, each constituency containing as close to the same number of voters as is practical.

(b) Each constituency would return three members to the National Assembly.

(c) Each voter would have two votes for individual candidates by whom the voter would like to be represented in the National Assembly. In addition, the voter would have one vote for a political party of his or her choice.

(d) Each political party would prepare a party list of candidates.

(e) 300 members would thus be directly elected by the constituencies, but 50 additional members would be elected from the national party lists, with a cut-off of 3 per cent in the first election, and subsequently of 5 per cent, to ensures proportional a reflection of voters' preferences as possible.

(f) The total number of registered voters will be about 22 million.

(g) The total number of people who will actually vote in a given election will probably be about 16 million (72 per cent)

(h) The National Assembly will have 300 members, and there will be 10 states.

(i) Each state will be entitled to roughly equal numbers of representatives in the National Assembly, and each state will have 1.6 million votes cast, and will be represented by 30 members.

(j) Each state will be divided into 10 constituencies for elections for the National Assembly, each with approximately 160,000 voters.

Proposals

(1) Each state will be divided into 50 wards (with approximately 32,000 people who exercise their vote in each), and each ward will elect six people.

(2) This multi-member election could take place on the following (alternative) bases:

(a) Each party would put up a maximum of three candidates, determined by the party, and offered to the voters on a list; or

(b) Each party would draw up a list, as provided in (a) but would be obliged to include at least one member of a minority ethnic group present in that ward; or

(c) The voter would have six votes, one per candidate; or

(d) The voter would have five, four or three votes, one per candidate; or

(e) The voter would have one vote only, either for a party list, contemplated in (a) or (b) or for one of the candidates.

The effect of these proposals would be that the voters would either vote for a party list, or would vote for six or less candidates, according to their preferences.

(3) The 300 people thus elected could then

(a) be the members of the legislative assembly of that state; and

(b) act as an electoral college to elect the 30 members to represent that state in the National Assembly

(4) The election of the 30 members by this 300-strong electoral college could be :

(a) preferably by means of the single transferable voting system; or

(b) on the basis of a list system. In such a case, the members of the electoral college would have 30 votes, and each party would submit a list of not more than 20 candidates, in the form of

(i) a closed list whereby the member of the electoral college simply votes for the party. In this case, the voter's vote for the closed list would amount to 20 votes, and he/she would then be entitled to use his other 10 votes for the list of another party if he/she so wishes; OR

(ii) an open list (i.e., the member of the electoral college is not presented with an ordered list, but with a series of names in alphabetical order). The voter can then vote by marking a space beside the candidate of his choice; he/she could then use the residue of the ten votes in respect of the list(s) of another Party if he/she so wishes; OR

(iii) a free list where the voter can cast his/her 30 votes for candidates of different parties, and can even culminate two votes for any one candidate if he/she so wishes.

Alternative 3

(1) The country is divided into 175 constituencies, each of roughly equal size.

(2) Each party presents to the voters a list of not more than 175 candidates, which forms the official list of the party. This list may also be drawn up on a federal basis, in which case the list would contain proportionately fewer candidates.

(3) Each voter has two votes one for a candidate who is standing for election in the constituency, and one for the party of his/her choice. The constituency representative is chosen by a simple majority of votes, and together with other constituency representatives, makes up half the membership of the National Assembly.

(4) The other 175 members of the National Assembly are elected on the basis of the number of votes cast for the party divided by the total number of votes cast for the various parties, expressed as a percentage. A party will be entitled to one representative off its list for every 0.57 per cent of the votes cast, subject to a 3 per cent cut-off in the first election of the National Assembly, and thereafter a 5 per cent cut-off.

The Democratic Party's Plan for South Africa

The Party commits itself to a true South African democracy which rejects race as its basis, which protects the human dignity and liberty of all its citizens, which promotes the general interest and which is founded on the principles which form the basis of liberal democracy. The protection of fundamental human rights and liberties, including freedom of speech, franchise association, private ownership, free elections, religion, language and culture. It supports a central government having limited authority and power. It strengthens the authorities in various sphere of government in order to bring the people closer to it. It favours more and maximum powers to the different provinces specially economic power along with the political one. It refers to an independent judiciary and the rule of law.

Human Rights and Role of Other Parties of South Africa

(1) Azanian People's Organization (AZAPO)

Drawing on the Africanist ideology formulated by Steve Biko in the Black Consciousness Movement in the 1970's and on revolutionary socialism, AZAPO positions itself on the far left. Capitalism and apartheid were one and the same thing for AZAPO. The two evils could not be separated in the struggle for liberation.[15]

AZAPO's refused to negotiate might increase its support among those who think that negotiations have given them too little. The organisation does not visible in the last two election polls. Cooper, a former AZAPO*s president, argues that the movement has failed to adjust to the fundamental changes that have taken place around it. Lacking a clear and realistic programme, the movement fails to attract support on radical principles alone, "Echoing empty military does not achieve results, however strident; rather, it serves to lose existing and potential support."[16]

AZAPO believes that AZANIA (South Africa) is a unitary state. Hence, AZAPO rejects the bulkanisation of AZANIA into separate semi-autonomous units. An AZAPO Government will seek to abolish provincial governments as presently constituted and consolidate the country into fewer provinces with administrative functions of government carrying out Central Government policies and directions.

AZAPO, uncompromisingly rejects all value systems that seek to make Black People foreigners in the land of their birth. This rejection is accompanied by a conscious efforts to define and fight for better future for the poor. When AZAPO refers to our country as AZANIA, it spells out its rejection of the name South Africa and its colonial connotations. For AZAPO, a new society should rename and need to be devoid of the legacy of apartheid. AZAPO believes that the conquered–conqueror relations between blacks and whites determined and continues to determine the ownership of land in the country.

2. South African Communist Party (SACP)

The Communist Party of South Africa (CPSA) was founded in 1921. It dissolved in 1950 when it was banned by the government. The South African Communist Party (SACP) was founded in secrecy in 1953 and worked closely with the ANC. The SACP's strategy was formulated as a two-phased revolution : the first phase was to support the ANC in its struggle for national liberation and once that had been accomplished, and the second phase was to turn South Africa into a socialist state. When the first phase seems close to realisation - however different from the vision held by the party the question that remains is how the party should realise the second phase in a future democracy. The SACP think that there is no transformation of society in South Africa. Prior to socialist revolution, it needs a democratic revolution. That's why SACP is one of the main partners of ANC in Central Government, but as a SACP it does not participate in the electoral politics. The SACP favours a unitary state having limited powers to the provinces. It recognises Reconstruction and Development Programme (RDP) document as instrument of social transformation. Overall, the ideas of federalism is not the choice of SACP.

3. Freedom Front (FF)

The Freedom Front was launched by General Constand Vilyoin in March 1994 following a split in the Afrikaner People's Front (APF) over the issue of participation in the April 1994 election, with the FF opting to register to present the case for a "white homeland". In late March the FF stated that its objectives was a confederal South Africa based on the "inalienable and non-negotiable", right of self-determination for Afrikaners and all other groups. Subsequent to the April 1994 poll, at which it placed fourth with 2.2 per cent of the vote. During the first election, electorates (mainly whites) were confused which gave FF chance to recognise its ideology. The people of South Africa has rejected the idea of FF during this election (June, 1999). The idea of 'Volkstaat' (Freestate) and the theory behind it has not recognised. The FF has been marginalised and its supporters are trying to manage themselves either in DP or NNP.

4. United Democratic Movement

Mover and Holomisa together established a new political party, the United Democratic Movement (UDM) in September 1997. The UDM manifesto said, "we will Unite South African from all communities is a new political home, built on the foundation of the principles and ideals of our national constitution."[17]

The UDM is a party born in the new South Africa, free from the politics of fear and coercion and the party said under a UDM government, South Africa will become a world class nation in ten years. A world class nation is one that offers a quality life to all its citizens, addressing the fundamental human needs for good, water, shelter and sanitation, as well as fulfilling every citizens constitutional right to a job, safety, adequate housing, equality, education and health care.

5. Pan-Africanist Congress

The PAC desires to Unite all Black South African in a single national front. Based at Lacaka, Zambia, the Congress announced in May 1979. The PAC won 12 per cent of the vote and five assembly seats in 1994 election.

The Constitution Making Process and Convention for a Democratic South Africa (CODESA)

South Africa took significant steps in the last mile of its journey from apartheid to freedom and democracy when the first convention for a democratic South Africa (CODESA) was held on 21st December 1991 in Johnnesburg. This was the beginning of an effort to work out a new democratic constitution for South Africa which would replace the existing apartheid-based constitution. Hence, 20th December 1991 was red letter day in the history of South Africa.

Prior to the CODESA meeting on 20th December 1991 there was a Preparatory Committee meeting on 29 and 30 November 1991. This preparatory Committee meeting was held after prolonged meetings among various political parties organization and the government. Originally, 20 political parties had attended the preparatory committee meeting but one of them, the Pan-Africanist Congress (PAC), withdrew from it on the second day, with the result that only 19 parties were left in the hold.

The preparatory committee decided to invite the following as guests to observe the proceedings of the CODESA :

(a) Heads of diplomatic missions

(b) Representative of the following organization :

 (1) United National Organization (UNO)

 (2) Organization of African Unity (OAU)

 (3) The Common Wealth (CW)

 (4) The European Community (EC)

 (5) The Non-aligned Movement (NAM)

Agenda of CODESA

The preparatory committee agreed upon the following agenda for CODESA:

(a) Creation of a climate for free political participation

(b) General constitutional principles

(c) Two future of the TBUC states

(d) Role of the International Community

(e) Implementation of decision of CODESA

(f) Transitional arrangement/interim government/ transitional authority.

The most important work that the CODESA did was the adoption of a declaration of intent. This declaration was prepared in one of the task groups of the steering committee in which there was a delegate from each of the political parties/government attending the CODESA.[18]

Over all, one may analyse the political parties finds that it can be divided broadly into three groups like centrist parties, left parties and right wing parties. The ANC, DP, NNP and IFP favours more or less a federal state. The ANC favours a highly centralised federal state having legs powers to provinces. But the Constitution of South Africa provides substantial powers to the provinces. The DP, NNP and IFP desire maximum devolution of power to the states. The demand of provincial Constitution has been recognized by the constitution. Western Cape has adopted its own constitution but the constitution of Kwa Zulu Natal has rejected by the constitutional court. The left parties support the ANC views on centralised state. The right wing parties think that South Africa is a socialist state. They need a separate "Volk tant" for Afrikaners. This ideology is clearly rejected by majority of population.

The Assessment

Elections are in themselve inadequate to creat democracy. There is a need of strong multi party system which incorporaties the features of democratic country. The first election of April 27, 1994 confirmed the idea of consolidation. The second election of June 1999 has confirmed the idea of multi party democratic country having divisions of powers. The provinces are playing their important role in the process of socio-economic development. Along with, it, the Judiciary is playing its independent role in the development of South Africa overall there is a need of stable government by which they can proceed for socio-economic development. It is clear that it depends upon particular party to interpret Constitution. Along with it, it is the policies of particular party by which one can develop the state.

References

1. O. Apter, *The Politics of Modernisation* (Chicago, University of Chicago x°ress, 1967), p. 179.
2. T. Hodge, South Africa : Democracy and development in a post apartheid society in F. Legtwitch ed. *Democracy and Development,* (Cambridge, Polity Press, 1996), p. 195.
3. Heather Deegan, *South Africa Reborn : Building a new Democracy* (London, UCL Press. 1999), p. 39.
4. African National Congress, 1994, Constitution, Marshaltown: ANC Department of Information and Publication, p. 4.
5. John Mukum Mbaku and Julius Othonobere, "South Africa's first democratic elections and their political content", in Frame Buntman ed. *Multiparty Democracy and Political Change* (England, Astegate Publishing Ltd., 1998), p. 245.
6. R.M. Price, *The Apartheid State in Crisis : Political Transformation in South Africa : 1975-1990* (New York, Oxford University Press, 1991), p. 99.
7. Heather Deegan, *op. cit.*, p. 50.
8. Heather Deegan *Ibid*, p. 53.
9. *Ibid.*, p. 58.
10. S.C. Saxena, South Africa : Walking the last Miles (Delhi, Kalinga Publication, 1992), p. 478.
11. S.C. Saxena, Ibid., p. 480.
12. *Ibid*, p. 481.
13. Inkatha Freedom Party, 1987, *Inkatha and the struggle for liberation in South Africa* (Durban, Inkatha Freedom Party, 1987), p. 46.

14. S.C. Saxena, *op. cit.*, p. 467.

15. T. Lodge, *op. cit.*, pp. 152-150.

16. S. Cooper, "What went wrong black consciousness", *The Weekly Mail*, 14- 20 May, 1993, p. 17.

17. South of Sahara, 1999, J.D. Omer-Coper, p. 983.

18. South of Sahara, p. 851.

4 Foreign Policy and Human Rights

Introduction

A writer has rightly stated that the foreign policy of a country depends on a whole series of factors acting simultaneously and not always in the same direction and that it is the sum of these factors which determines and guides the foreign policy of a country. This implies that in order to understand the foreign policy of a country, it is necessary to collect a large number of heterogeneous factors which have a direct, or even indirect, influence upon its foreign policy. This itself is a difficult task. After collecting the large number of factors, we have to proceed to analyze each one of them carefully with a view to discovering the degree of influence which each of them, singly or in conjunction with other factors, exercises in determining the contours of the foreign policy of a country. As a result of this exercise, we are likely to come to the conclusion that each relevant factor does not, and possibly can not, exercise equal amount of, or same degree of, influence on the foreign policy of a country. We would find that some factors exercise more, and some less, and some insignificant, influence in the formulation of the foreign policy of a country. It is also important to study; all the relevant factors in their historical development because of the fact that 'a factor which takes precedence over all the others in a particular set of circumstances will moderate when those circumstances change and give way to other factors.'[1]

Apart from these difficulties, further difficulties arise because of the fact that international politics is a complex phenomenon, and it is not easy to define it. This is because of excessive interaction between the domestic and international fields due to which the distinction between home and foreign policies of a country, for all practical purposes, has become almost blurred. 'Internal factors project into international politics, and external factors have their repercussions on home affairs.' Thus, it is difficult to distinguish between the internal and external factors and to say which factor relates inclusively to the international field. These problems arise in respect of all the countries, big or small, rich or poor, militarily weak or strong, newly independent states, or states independent since long.

In connection with the question of internal and external determinants of the foreign policy of a state, we may mention the views of Professor F. S. Northedge also who stated that the aims of the foreign policy of a country are the products of interaction between pressures which are both internal and external to the state. He has also said that 'foreign policy...is an interplay between the outside and the inside.'[2] If this is true, the problem that arise is as to how to identify these internal and external factors. This is by no means an easy task. Professor Joseph Frankel, however, seems to solve this problem when he says that, though the environment of foreign policy decisions is limitless embracing as it does the whole of the universe, yet in practice the environment is circumscribed by the range of interests; and the limitation of power of every single state act as general limiting factors.[3]

We should bear in mind that South Africa in particular and the African states in general, because of their economic and military weakness, do not dream of dominating world. Thus, while safeguarding their global and strategic interest is one of the important constraints on internal determinants of the foreign policy of superpowers; it is not so in the case of small and economically weak states of Africa. This does not mean that the states of Africa do not have any interest in world peace, nor does it mean that they are not affected by tension anywhere in the world. However, the question of global peace, important though it might be for them, cannot be one of the important determinants of the foreign policies of African states for the simple reason that they are militarily and economically too weak to be able to exercise significant influence upon the war and peace questions facing the world.[4]

Therefore, the major areas of interest of the African states mostly be either within their own boundaries or within the continent of Africa. Internally, the main concerns of the African states are with unity, stability, independence and economic development of their countries. These internal needs of the African countries act as important determinants of their foreign policies. Externally, the African states are mostly concerned only with problems that are immediate concern to them as African states. Thus, we see that the issues and problems, which are of immediate interest or concern to the African states, are mostly African.[5]

In trying to identify internal and external factor affecting the foreign policies of the African states, we may conveniently group these variables or determinants under two major headings – the "domestic setting", and the 'Internal environment". In the category of "domestic setting", we can place such factors as the state of economy and the potential for development, sources for internal political pressure and the role of governing elites. In the category of "external environment", we can place the three important external determinants, that is, their geographical location, and the existence of colonialism and white supremacist regimes. It may be mentioned that, since South Africa is an African state, it is not immune from the influence of the aforesaid variables upon its foreign policies.

Domestic Setting of Foreign Policy

The domestic setting, as stated earlier, includes three important variables or determinants, namely, the economic condition and potential for economic development, the degree of internal political pressure through various pressure groups and the role of elites.[6] We will examine them briefly.

State of Economy

Though many African states are quite rich in economic resources, their peoples are suffering under the yoke of poverty. The fault for this state of affairs lies with the colonial powers. They did not bring about an all-round economic development of their colonies. Whatever economic development that took place in the colonies during the colonial era followed three set courses.

Firstly, they ensured through their policies that their colonies remained exporters of primary produce only, particularly those things which they needed for their own industries. They did not set up any major industries in their colonies lest they should absorb those produce themselves. This was done because they wanted them to remain importers of finished goods and manufactures from them so that their own industries might flourish.

Secondly, the colonial powers ensured that the colonies by and large remained dependent on a single crop as far as agriculture was concerned.

Thirdly, they ensured that the bulk of their colonies' trade remained only with Europe and North America. They did not encourage intra-African trade which, therefore, failed to flourish at all during the colonial era.

Not only was the trade of the African countries largely with their former colonial masters, but their entire economy including their currency was also tied to their currency during the colonial era. Such was the extent of the stranglehold exercised by the colonial powers over the economy of their colonies when they granted them independence, and that situation has not changed appreciably even many decades after their independence.

Till the economic stranglehold of the colonial powers is shaken off, or loosened considerably, by the African states and they no able to reach self-generating take-off stage in their economic development, the African states will have to conduct their foreign policy under severe strain exercised upon them by the need to bring about an accelerated economic development which has to be given top priority. Because of severe economic compulsions, many African states have been compelled to make concessions on political front in one form or the other hoping to secure some tangible economic benefits. All this shows that the economic constraints upon each newly independent African state is certainly very powerful.

Internal Political Pressure

Another important determinant of the foreign policy of African states is the political pressure exercised by various groups of people within their border. It is true that the African states do not have organized pressure groups or lobbies as they exist in Western Europe and America. Nevertheless, there are some very important pressure groups in African states also, and they do exercise significant influence upon their foreign policies. The pressure groups include the military, political groups within the ruling party, youth organizations, ethnic and tribal groups and trade unions.[7]

In a large number of African states, the military has taken over the government of their country and are in effective command in all spheres of public life there. Military, as a pressure group is however, an important source of influence even in those states where it is not in power because their advice in matters of 'direct professional concern' cannot be ignored by any responsible government of any country. By and large, the influence of military has been generally of a conservative character, particularly in the foreign policy sphere. It is in relations with the major powers that the military exercises greatest influence. Since most of the African military leaders were trained in the military academies of their former colonial masters, they want their country to lean on their former rulers not only for the supply of military hardware for their army but also for the training of their personnel.

The other group which often exercises significant influence upon the foreign policy is that of youths who have their own nationwide organizations in many countries. This group is more aggressive than other groups. Then, there are some ethnic and tribal groups also in almost all African countries, and these groups too exercise tremendous influence upon the foreign policy, especially where they are politically quite powerful.

The Colonial Heritage

One of the most important factors determining the foreign relations of African states is their colonial history and colonial heritage. Colonial heritage means all those links–social, economic, political and cultural - which were forged or unconsciously grew up between the colonial power and its colony. At the time of their independence, the African states found themselves entangled in a highly intricate web of such links. The implication of these links is that, while political independence has been attained by the African states, they, for all practical purposes, continue to be still chained to their former colonial masters as a result of these links. The most important of these links are those of language, culture, currency, legal and judicial system, educational pattern, administrative organization etc. Each colonial power introduced its own language in its colonies. The few natives of the colonies who were fortunate enough to receive higher education were made to study the literature, history and biographies of the great men of their colonial masters. All this amounted to a sort of cultural invasion of the colonies because the natives were always taught to hate their own culture, language, tribal practices etc, and to love those of their colonial masters.

The colonial powers also linked the currencies of their colonies with their own, which enabled them to control the economy of their colonies. They also introduced their own laws and legal systems into their colonies. No colony, on gaining independence, could possibly think of breaking these links for fear of paralyzing the economy of the country. The African states did not, and possibly could not, scrap the economic links with their erstwhile colonial masters because they found them useful.[8]

It is obvious that such visible and invisible links of African states with their former colonial powers, as have been cited above, should influence their foreign policies, particularly when they can not break them or do not want to break them because of the benefits they receive in return. This situation may continue for a long time to come.[9]

The Governing Elites

The nature of the governing elites is also a powerful determinant of the foreign policy of African states. In most of these countries, the field of foreign affairs is a special preserve of the Presidents who are quite powerful. This is mainly because of two reasons: *firstly,* most African states are still to carve out for themselves established interests in the international arena because they are new within the international system. Consequently, there is nothing like the traditional pattern of external behaviour as one finds in the older established states. *Secondly,* there are no serious domestic institutional restraints on the behaviour of the African rulers. Hence, we find that in most cases the President acts as his own Foreign Minister. Even when there is a Foreign Minister, he acts as "his courier" rather than an important figure in the formulation of foreign policy.

This does not mean that the Presidents of the African states, who are also the foreign policy-makers, can act in disregard, or even in defiance, of the external constraints. The constraints are, no doubt, there but the choice open to them is extremely limited, with the result that a change in President does not necessarily result in drastic changes in the foreign policy of that country.[10]

External Environment

In the external environment, the most powerful determinants are: the geographical situation of the country concerned, the existence of colonialism and white supremacist regimes, and the Cold War environment. We will now examine each of these determinants briefly.

Geographical Location

The geographical location of a state is an important determinant of its foreign policy. The special thing about this determinant is that, unlike other determinants, it is permanent and unchangeable.[11] The foreign policy of a state may possibly show some variation under various governments but they would never be formulated in complete disregard of the geographical compulsions.

The geography of a country as a determinant of its foreign policy is important also because it conditions and influences ether factors also. For instance, the latitudinal and longitudinal location of a country in the world determines its climate, including its temperatures and rainfall, all of which affect agricultural production. In other words, the economic parameters of a country are largely determined by its climate. The economic structure of a country decides whether, and to what extent, it would be dependent upon other countries. A country with starvation staring in the face of its people can not be bold and adventurous in its foreign relations. In other words, it will be compelled to subordinate its policies to its economic needs.

The location of a country determines its potential allies as well as its enemies. A country like Iceland, for example, has absolutely nothing to fear from a distantly located country like China. However, a country like India which shares its border with China has no alternative but to shape its defence policies and military preparedness in the light of the military prowess of China. To take another example, Egypt's foreign policy is not going to be influenced by developments in South Africa which is situated on the southern tip of the continent, but Botswana, a next door neighbour of South Africa will have to exercise severe restraint and caution while dealing with its big neighbour.

In connection with the consideration of the geographical situation of a country as a determinant of the foreign policy, one more question arises, that is, whether the state is a landlocked one or a littoral one. If it is landlocked, it would always be at the mercy of one or more of its neighbouring countries which are not landlocked. This view assumes special significance in view of the fact that the bulk of the foreign trade of landlocked African countries cannot be carried on in the absence of a sea port. It, therefore, becomes incumbent upon the landlocked states to maintain, as far as possible, cordial relations with the neighbouring countries through whose territories the imports and exports have to pass.

Existence of Colonialism and White Supremacist Regimes

Until recently, the foreign policies of African states used to be influenced by their commitment to wipe out every trace of colonialism and racism from the continent. Every African state was determined to take this struggle to its logical conclusion. Many of these states, particularly those situated in Southern Africa had to pay a very heavy price for supporting the struggle against colonialism and racism at the hands of racist South Africa. Now this factor has ceased to be a determinant of their foreign policy because all African countries have acceded to independence, and *apartheid* has met its demise in South Africa, thanks to the marathon efforts made by the people of the country backed by the international community.

The Cold War Environment

This factor is no longer valid because the Cold War is over. However, when the Cold War was at its peak, the foreign policies of most African states were affected by this phenomenon. During the hey-day of the Cold War, the world was divided into two hostile camps – the Western bloc and the Soviet bloc. The birth of the non-aligned movement in 1961 gave the opportunity to the newly independent states not to align with either of these blocs. Africa is the only continent in the world which is totally non-aligned. Even the Charter of the Organization of African Unity (OAU) enjoins upon all African countries to follow the non-aligned path, which they readily do. By following the non-aligned policy, the African states were able to draw aid and assistance from both the blocs without tying themselves politically with any of the blocs. Many states turned to the Soviet bloc when they could not get the required aid from the Western bloc.

Determinants of the South African Foreign Policy

During the *apartheid* era, the sole concern of the South African government was to follow a foreign policy that guaranteed the continuance of the *apartheid*. With this end in view, it forged wide-ranging relationship with western countries, nationalist government of China based in Taiwan, and Israel. South Africa became a major area for western investments. Hundreds of multinationals and other companies made sizeable investments in South Africa. Military ties with the West were also forged. So, defence of *apartheid* became the sole determinant of South Africa's foreign policy. The West was also interested in the preservation of *apartheid* in South Africa as long as it was possible because it was also reaping enormous profits from the practice of racial policies by the South African government.

Again, it was the need to preserve *apartheid* that led South Africa to adopt hostile posture towards the neighbouring black states who were staunch supporters of the struggle led by the ANC to bring about the demise of *apartheid*.

Other factors did not influence the foreign policy of South Africa during *apartheid* years. South Africa is not a landlocked state and, therefore, its imports and exports did not depend on the mercy of the neighbouring states. On the contrary, some of the neighbouring landlocked states were at the mercy of South Africa for their imports and exports. Economically also, South Africa was well placed *vis-a-vis* the neighbouring states. Most of its exports went to the western world, nationalist China and Israel. Even the neighbouring black states were buying the essential goods from South Africa because they had no other option. Buying from distant countries would have been very expensive for them, and their frail economies could not afford high cost of goods. A large number of migrant labourers from the neighbouring countries worked in South Africa, but this factor worked to the disadvantage of the countries from which the workers originated. For them, it was a source of income through the remittances sent by their nationals working in South Africa.

After the demise of *apartheid* and the installation of a black-ruled government in South Africa, the priorities of the country have changed. It has no need to adopt hostile policy towards the neighbouring states which had provided solid support to the struggle against *apartheid*. Now, the black-ruled states expect South Africa to help them in the gigantic task of national reconstruction and economic development. This expectation is based on the fact that South Africa is the most developed nation of Southern Africa. Unfortunately, it is not possible for South Africa to meet all the development requirements of the neighbouring countries. This is because South Africa needs lot of money for development within its own borders for the benefit of its huge black population which had remained deprived during the *apartheid era*. Still, South Africa's emergence as a black-ruled state is a great boon for the Southern African Development Community (SADC).

For South Africa, the Southern African region has become a region of priority. Nelson Mandela and other South African leaders have clearly stated that the first priority for South Africa is the Southern African region followed by the rest of the continent. It is natural for the South African leaders to give priority to the Southern African region because South Africa's own development would be accelerated with the development taking place in the neighbouring countries.

South Africa's economic and trade links with the West, developed during the *apartheid* era, can not be snapped by the black majority government. It needs to promote, rather than curtail, trade with the West because it needs money for its own development and for providing employment to millions of unemployed youths in the country. In fact, the economic compulsions are so great that South Africa is trying to tap new markets for the expansion of its exports. Even with the nationalist China, with which it has snapped diplomatic relations, it is maintaining economic relations.

In the political sphere, the black-ruled government of South Africa has no compulsion toe the western line. Hence, it is taking an independent line based on merit of the issue. For example, Nelson Mandela visited Libya in spite of the opposition of the western states.

In short, we can say that foreign policy constraints for South Africa are now quite different from what they were during the *apartheid*. This is why we see a dramatic turn in its foreign policy. In some respects, of course, we see some continuity also as, for example, in the continuance of the economic relations with the West. The post-*apartheid* South Africa is going to play a very important role in international relations. Nelson Mandela has been elected Chairman of the Non-Aligned Movement. His presence at the top of this powerful organization may result in the new direction being given to some of the most burning issues of the day.

New South Africa's Foreign Policy and Human Rights

After a prolonged armed struggle under the leadership of the ANC, and international support, South Africa was finally able to get rid of *apartheid*. After the first democratic and multi-party elections held in April 1994, a Government of National Unity headed by Nelson Mandela was sworn in. The new government then set upon the task of framing the domestic and foreign policies which should be in line with the aims, interests and aspirations of the people. The task of framing the foreign policy of the democratic South Africa was, however, not easy. It was realized that South Africa could not possibly afford to completely reverse the foreign policy that was being followed by the previous government.

As we know, the South African government, under the *apartheid* regime, was following a pro-western foreign policy that was necessitated by the desire of the racist government to protect and defend its *apartheid-based* political and economic structure.

However, in the process South Africa had forged wide-ranging economic relations with the Western countries. These relations could not be snapped because severing economic relations with the Western countries would bring about a complete collapse of the economy of the country. Hence, economic relations would have to continue with the Western countries in the interest of the country. The new South African rulers realized that, although the Western countries had supported the racist regime, economic relations would still have to be retained with them. So, in that sense, there would have to be some continuity in the foreign policy of the country.

The most immediate terrain of foreign policy for the new South Africa in which policy shifts would be closely watched, as the South African leaders calculated, was the African sub-continent where the country was situated, it was felt that the "new" South Africa, in its foreign affairs, would have to be less Euro-centric as it used to be under *apartheid,* so that it could pay more attention to the African continent and: within the continent, to Southern African region. Here a drastic change in foreign policy would have to be effected.

As we know, during the *apartheid* era, the neighbouring states of South Africa were treated virtually as "enemies" because they were providing support to the liberation movements. These states would have to be extended a hand of friendship and cooperation. Besides, they would have to be given assurance that the "new" South Africa was their friend who could be depended for economic development and national security.

The South African leaders were conscious of the expectations from the new government - expectations of African countries as a whole and the neighbouring states in particular. African countries expected South Africa to take a leading role in the promotion of human rights and democracy in the continent. This expectation was based on the fact that the struggle against *apartheid* in South Africa was basically a struggle for human rights and democracy. Since this struggle had been successfully won, the African states expected the "new" South Africa to work for the restoration of human rights and democracy in the rest of the continent. The big question was whether South Africa could serve as the hope of the continent.

These and other foreign policy considerations were part of the evolution of a new political order which led to a redefinition of priorities, including re-valuation of foreign policy objectives of the "new" government. In the light of democratic South Africa's perceived strengths and weaknesses, identifiable challenges constituted the country's eVolving foreign policy. These were:[12]

- formulating a foreign policy framework based on national consensus.
- reaching clarity on South Africa's stance on human rights.
- reconstructing South Africa's leadership role in Southern Africa; and
- analyzing the question of multilateral relations and the global economy, including promotion of positive South African relations with "pariah" States.

In sum, the critical questions facing the formative stages of South Africa's foreign policy require some revisiting. Amplified, these include the country's key foreign policy objectives: its positioning *vis-a vis* Africa, Europe, the USA and the Middle East: the criteria to be used to choose between China and Taiwan, resurrecting South Africa's policy on Nigeria, prioritizing international forums to promote the country, and, not the least, relations with countries like Libya, Cuba and Iran without alienating the United States and other Western powers.[13] The response of South Africa to these issues will be discussed in subsequent chapters. The South African leaders realized that they would have to do all that they can to reverse the isolation which their country was pushed into by the *apartheid* regime. Further, they would have to take steps to roll back the years of foreign relations damage caused by white rule, and would have to search for proper direction and a pro-active foreign policy approach.[14]

Several issues regarded as "cornerstones" of the foreign policy of the "new" South Africa were identified: human rights, democracy, justice, peace, Africa, and economic development. South Africa's newly acquired membership of the Commonwealth, the United Nations, the G-77, the OAU, the SADC, the Non-Aligned Movement, the UNCTAD, the ILO, the WHO, and the UNICEF were bound to, facilitate these objectives.

In 1994, South Africa was a lonely, isolated country with reputation for beating up its neighbours and a belligerent attitude to the rest of Africa. Its first priority was to create relations that were acceptable - relations of friendship, cooperation, and good neighbourliness. The first foreign policy objective - that of persuading a skeptical Africa of South Africa's good intentions - led to the government's initial foreign affairs act of joining the Organization of African Unity (OAU). As if to move away from being regarded by Africa as an extension of Europe, South Africa also joined its regional neighbours in the Southern Africa Development Community (SADC).

Setting Foreign Policy Priorities

The South African foreign policy-makers felt that it was desirable to establish a general understanding of the values on which decisions and standpoints were premised. It was also important to establish a clear chain of command, throughout which there would be an acceptance of South Africa's role in the international community, and the eVolving nature of that community.

The *Foreign Policy Discussion Document* published by the South African government made clear that what was required in South Africa was a notion what South Africa's foreign policy priorities should be some form of ranking of priorities, and also the setting of an orderly and systematic manner of achieving these. The two priorities could be as follows:[15]

- Encouraging stability and development to Southern Africa; and
- Securing incremental improvements in investment and trade links worldwide.

These strategic "pillars" of the foreign policy of South Africa eVolved tactically, in turn:

- keeping South Africa's established trading and investment partners on-side;
- encouraging new links with emerging markets in the Asia-Pacific and Latin American regions and elsewhere;
- representing the interests of Southern Africa in international fora; and
- extending assistance to the region where necessary in the interests of stability and development.

In practice, this mean that in the near future, South Africa's foreign policy priorities would have to include:

- Fleshing out the Southern Development Community (SADC);
- Concluding an arrangement with the European Union on a Free Trade Protocol;
- Renegotiating the Southern African Customs Union (SACU) Agreement;
- Encouraging stability and reform in Africa, especially in Southern Africa and, further a field, in Nigeria. This will be part and parcel of South Africa's contribution to Thabo Mbeki's vision of 'African renaissance';
- Developing a position on U.N. reforms;
- Attempting to reinvigorate the Non-aligned Movement of which South Africa was to assume the chairmanship in 1998; and
- Continuing to develop trade and investment links.

According to President Mandela, the pillars upon which South Africa's foreign policy will rest are the following beliefs:[16]

- that issues of human rights are central to international relations and an understanding that they extend beyond the political, embracing the economic, social and environmental;
- that just and lasting solutions to the problems of humankind can only come through the promotion of democracy worldwide;
- that consideration of justice and respect for international law should guide the relations between nations;
- that peace is the goal for which all nations should strive, and where this breaks down, internationally agreed and non-violent mechanism, including effective arms-control regime, must be employed;
- that the concerns and interests of the continent of Africa should be reflected in our foreign policy choices; and
- that economic development depends on growing regional and international economic cooperation in an interdependent world.

It is obvious that South Africa cannot ignore the fact that it is situated in the continent of Africa comprising a group of 54 countries which had stood solidly behind the struggle against *apartheid.* Therefore, in its foreign policy there will have to be focus on Africa, though care will have to be taken to balance this against other demands and priorities.[17] Trade with Africa amounted to 8.3 per cent of the overall total in 1995; with the European Union (EU), 33 per cent; with the North American Free Trade Area (NAFTA - Mexico, the United States, and Canada), 9 per cent; with the states of Latin America's Mercosur grouping, 1.7 per cent; with Asia and the Middle East, 26 per cent; and with member states of the Southern African Customs Union (Botswana, Namibia, Lesotho and Swaziland), 8.5 per cent.[18]

President Mandela has argued that 'South Africa can not escape its African destiny. If we do not devote our energies to this continent, we too could fall victim to the forces that have brought ruin to its various parts.'[19] Aside from improvements in relations in the more obvious areas of political and security interaction, there has also been a tremendous growth in South Africa's trade and investment ties with the African sub-continent.

Nelson Mandela has argued that because of its relatively strong economy, and the legacy of *apartheid,* South Africa has a responsibility to help develop the region. Moreover, Mandela has pronounced strong Pan-Africanist sentiments claiming that "because I am an African the emphasis of South African relations should be on promoting peace and the elimination of poverty. In forging links with our neighbours, the ANC will draw on an African tradition, of which we are a part, of promoting greater continental unity." South Africa has quite a different outlook and view of its neighbours under the new government. The new South African government views its neighbours as friends, and Southern Africa is a first priority.[20]

The new government's regional policies are based upon the following principles of foreign policy:

- The collective nature of the construction of a new regional order.
- An anti-militaristic and development-oriented approach to regional security and cooperation.
- South Africa's renunciation of all hegemonic regional ambitions. The South African government believes that unless South Africa achieves mutually beneficial development in Southern African region, it will not be able to tackle effectively its international or regional challenges.[21]

South Africa's foreign policy with regard to Southern African region reflects a commitment to close diplomatic, economic and security, cooperation, adherence to human rights, promotion of democracy as well as regional solidarity. The states of Southern Africa share a common destiny. The primary objective of the democratic government of South Africa is to promote regional cooperation by maximizing growth and national welfare, leading eventually to sustained regional development and economic integration. President Mandela is of the opinion: "None of us can achieve sustainable growth and development, or peace and stability in isolation." In June 1994, President Mandela attended his first Frontline States Summit in Harare as Head of State of South. Africa. This Summit reviewed the future of the Frontline States in the light of South Africa's transition to democracy.

South Africa's foreign policy with regard to Botswana, Lesotho, Namibia and Swaziland (the BLNS countries) is based on the following principles:

- political good neighbourliness;
- promotion of mutual cooperation, trade and sustained economic growth in the context of the South African Customs Union (SACU) and the Southern Africa Development Community (SADC);
- introduction of effective cross-border control mechanism to solve problems relating to stock-theft, drug and arms smuggling; and
- promotion of mutual cooperation and interaction in social and cultural fields.

Bilateral relations with the BLNS countries are good and growing steadily in the above-mentioned fields. Relations are also conducted on diplomatic level and are based on mutual interest, respect, friendliness and constructive approach.[22] In security matters, plans are now well advanced for the former Frontline States to reconstitute themselves into a new Voluntary association of Southern African states whose purpose will be to respond rapidly and effectively to any threat to the peace, security, and democratic development of the sub-continent.[23]

The South African government also provides technical assistance and financial assistance to needy Southern African countries. Four key pillars for sustainable growth and development come under technical programme. They are:

(a) Investing in people on the productive and creative core of the economy

In pursuance of this principle, South Africa has taken the following concrete measures to help the neighbouring countries:

- Three training centres have been established in Mozambique to develop basic skills and more than 1,000 trainees there have successfully completed courses.
- Assistance was given to Swaziland to establish two training centres - one of them concentrating on agricultural courses.
- Two skills training centres were established, one in Angola and one in Lesotho.
- More than 250 instructors from countries in the region have been trained in South Africa.
- Public, servants in neighbouring countries receive regular in-service training in South Africa.

(b) Creating employment in the region

The massive unemployment prevailing in the black states of Southern Africa is a problem for which no solution seems to be in sight. All African states are engaged in finding a solution to this problem but so far without any result. To achieve this objective, the South African government has taken the following measures in relation to the neighbouring countries:

- Citizens from neighbouring countries (Mozambique, Angola, Swaziland and Lesotho) have been trained in basic civil construction-related courses to start their own business.

- An industrial park has been established in Maputo (Lesotho).

(c) Crime prevention and security

In this respect, several neighbouring countries have been helped by South Africa in the following way:

- Mozambique has been supplied with vehicles and equipment to combat cross-border crime.[24]
- Customs and excise officials from Swaziland. Mozambique and Zambia have been trained to improve their on-the-job skills.

(d) Transforming government into an efficient and responsible instrument

This is undoubtedly a difficult task but South Africa has not been found wanting in this field also. It has taken the following measures in this field:

Neighbouring governments are assisted by seconded South African experts to strengthen their administrative ability.

Logistic monitoring and administrative support was given to assist the process of democratization in Angola, Mozambique and Lesotho.

South Africa and the countries of Southern Africa have developed bilateral relations through exchange of high level delegations. General cooperation agreements have been signed with the neighbouring countries with special care to ensure that implementation of various programmes.

In an endeavour to overcome the shortage of funds, the government of South Africa has embarked upon a programme to promote trilateral cooperation. The concept involves three parties: the recipient country, the donor and South Africa.

South Africa is well placed to provide the necessary implementation capacity as a result of technology and expertise developed for, and adapted to, African circumstances.[25]

South Africa and the Western Powers

South Africa's relations with the Western states have been deep and far-reaching. These were especially forged during the *apartheid* period when there were massive investments by western governments, companies and multinational corporations. South Africa's economy would have collapsed but for the help provided by the western governments, sometimes openly and sometimes clandestinely. It was because of the all-out support of the western states that the demise of *apartheid* and the independence of Namibia got delayed. The ANC of South Africa and the SWAPO of Namibia were never recognized by the western states, as they were described as communist organizations determined to cause destabilization in Southern Africa. However, these very liberation movements came to power in South Africa and Namibia much against the wishes of the western governments.

The relations between South Africa and the western governments developed in the *post-apartheid* period against the aforesaid background. It may not be possible to discuss South Africa's relations in the *post-apartheid* period with all the western governments due to paucity of space. Hence, we shall take up only two western countries - the United States and Britain. South Africa's relations with other western countries were, by and large, also on the same lines.

(a) South African policy towards the United States

Before April 1994, the United States maintained a virtually one dimensional relationship with South Africa, focusing on the domestic oppression and internationally destabilizing effects of *apartheid.* Bilateral agreements were allowed to lapse; trade and investment were discouraged by sanctions; and American aid was delivered only through non-governmental organizations. The United States did not consult South Africa on many international issues outside the region.

The democratic transition in South Africa evoked warm response in the United States. Since the transition, the South

African-US relationship has rapidly become richer and more complex. Mandela as a person enjoys wide reputation and is admired in the United States as a symbol of *anti-apartheid* struggle. The United States and the Mandela government are in fundamental agreement on such issues as promoting democracy, human rights, peaceful resolution of conflicts and the non-proliferation of weapons of mass destruction. This partnership between the two countries is important. South Africa, under the new government, has played an important role in negotiations leading to the indefinite extension of the Treaty on the Non-proliferation of Nuclear Weapons, has used its prestige and influence to help in restoring peace in Mozambique and Angola and has pressed for a return to democracy in Nigeria and has also made efforts to contain ethnic strife in Burundi.[26]

Mandela has succeeded in reinforcing Congressional opposition to the early removal of sanctions. In November 1993, both Mandela and de Klerk let it be known that it was in the national interest of new South Africa to have a close and favourable relationship with the United States. Since April 1994 a mutually beneficial relationship has developed between South Africa and the United States. The United States is already South Africa's biggest trading partner. In 1993 South Africa was America's 36 r largest export market. In 1994, the Trade and Industry Minister, Trevor Manuel, and the United States' Commerce Secretary, Ron Brown, signed an agreement establishing the United States and South Africa (inter-governmental Committee which would facilitate the development of commercial relations and related economic matters between the two countries.[27]

An agreement which aimed at increasing the Volume of products, services and investments moving between South Africa and the United States, was also concluded. A new US-South African Business Development Committee was formed to look at investments, in September 1994, the South African government signed its first bilateral agreement with the US Agency for International Development (AID) inVolving 9 million US dollar in aid for the administration of justice. In the same month the US AID undertook to facilitate the availability of R162 million of aid for low-cost housing in South Africa.

In October 1994, after a visit to the United States by President Mandela, the following assistance programme was announced:

(a) a 100 million US dollar Southern African Enterprise Development Fund – of which 50 million US dollars will be spent in South Africa – to boost small enterprise.

(b) a contribution of 50 million US dollars will be made to South Africa to boost small enterprises.

(c) a contribution of 50 million US dollars to help bring electricity to the townships.

(d) a 30 million US dollar aid to support basic health-care in South Africa.

(e) an agreement to launch the US Peace Corps in South Africa to help developmental initiatives in the country.

The then US Secretary of Agriculture, Mike Espy, arrived in South Africa in October 1994 to sign a joint agreement, providing technical assistance for rural development, school nutrition and water supplies.

The US has been fairly liberal in its financial aid to South Africa. In terms of grants and loans guarantees, the US AID plans to spend approximately 230 million US dollars in loan guarantee, of which 170 million US dollars were to be committed for the period 1994 to 1996. Assistance in the field of trade and commerce varies, and an amount of 80 million US dollar has been set aside in loan guarantee for these fields. In November 1994, the US AID donated R175 million for tertiary educational projects.[28]

President Mandela's October 1994 visit to Washington served to strengthen relationship with the US. Mandela noted the great deal of commonality in the goals and interests of South Africa and the United States and predicted that the relationship 'can only grow'. This relationship is, in the words of a State Department official, "a very important one" in which "we have many areas of potential cooperation" between the two countries. The two countries concluded an agreement for nuclear cooperation in September 1995. This agreement allows for the transfer of nuclear research and nuclear power production technology.

A joint United States-South Africa Binational Commission dealing with various aspects of the US-South Africa relations was established in 1995 under the chairmanship of Deputy President Thabo Mbeki and the Vice-President of the United States, Al-Gore. The launching of this Commission illustrates how bilateral relationship is growing closer between the two countries, following the demise of *apartheid.* South Africa's Foreign Minister, Alfred Nzo said in his budge speech of 24 April 1997 that the Binational Commission "is the most visible manifestation of our close bilateral relations with the United States which have been systematically developed and expanded over the last two years." It is also a token of recognition by the United States of South Africa's international importance and potential. The US has set up such Binational Commission with only three other countries Russia, Mexico and Egypt. The first meeting of the Commission took place in March 1995 in Washington; it was followed by the second meeting in Pretoria in December of that year. According to the Department of Foreign Affairs of South Africa, the Binational Commission meetings have led to the development of closer ties between the two countries in spheres such as trade agriculture, science and technology education energy and combating crime. As to trade between South Africa and the United States, it is currently worth 4.2 billion US dollars.[29] Given the Clinton Administration's overall intentions for a new continent-wide policy on American trade and investment in Africa, there is an on-going discussion on the expansion of the present US-South Africa Binational Commission to cover even security issues.[30]

Inevitably there are differences between the two countries also. South Africa, for historical reasons related to its liberation struggle, views relations with Cuba, Iran and Libya much differently than the United States does. For example, South Africa does not support the American economic embargo of Iran and so the United States is disappointed.[31] They are friends who were with us when we were alone", Mandela explained, and he added: "The enemies of the Western countries are not my enemies. And I am not prepared to have my conduct dictated by anyone at all."[32] However, Mandela's South Africa shows no intention of selling arms to, or cooperating on, nuclear production with Iran or any other country that threatens the peace. Trade issues also arise when the two countries have, as the United States and South Africa now do, a 4.2 billion US dollar trade relationship. These issues need to be addressed since they not only affect trade and investment but are also indicative of how rapidly South Africa is moving to liberalize its economy. A more contentious issue relates to indictment in the United States of several South African entities that allegedly violated US arms export control laws.

None of these issues can be ignored despite the emphasis over South Africa's transition. They must be addressed frankly, but with care to preserve the fundamental value and strength of the relationship. There is much to be gained, including learning new ways of achieving racial harmony in both societies.[33]

South Africa and Britain

The South Africa and British connection required careful handling by both Great Britain and South Africa. It has been a unique association which could not be claimed by any other former British colony on the African continent. Links did not break or weaken even after the Union of South Africa gained independence from Britain in 1910. However, a measure of strain appeared in the 1960s. Two developments about that time led to the mounting of tension between Britain and South Africa. On the one side was the international opposition to *apartheid,* which Britain could not entirely ignore, and, on the other, there appeared the internationalist trend among the Afrikaner-speaking leaders of the National Party which was a cause of anxiety about the socio-economic position of the {English-speaking) white population. South Africa's withdrawal from the Commonwealth in March 1961 symbolized the nature of tension between Britain and South Africa.[34]

However, today the Republic of South Africa has strong trade relations with Britain. South Africa is Britain's largest single trading partner in Africa. Annual trade amounts to some Rand 5 billion each way. Some estimates put the current value of British investments in South Africa at around Rand 35 billion; this large figure represents approximately half of all oversea investment in the Republic. There is a military and strategic dimension too, though its nature and importance keep changing. South Africa is a supplier of some strategic minerals and their alloys to Britain: chromium, manganese and platinum. Britain imports from South Africa about two-thirds of its chromium requirement, half of the manganese needs, and about one-third of platinum it uses. This factor has further strengthened the relationship between the two countries.

At the inauguration of Mandela's presidency, the British delegation was led by Prince Philip Anglo-South African relations were further cemented by Prime Minister John Major's visit in September 1994, the Queen's visit in March 1995, and President Mandela's visit to the United Kingdom in July 1996. There has been a steady two-way flow of important personalities of the two countries. South Africa is no more a white minority-ruled country, but "family association" has in a way been restored between the two countries after Mandela took over.

In July 1994, Britain unveiled a 100 million pounds aid package over three-year period to South Africa. A Memorandum of Development Cooperation was signed by Britain and South Africa in September 1994. The two governments agreed that British aid should be directed into five main areas to support Pretoria's Reconstruction and Development Programme. The five areas are: education, good governance, health, rural development and small enterprise development. The South African government has also signed an investment protection agreement with the United Kingdom government.[35]

In the *posi-apartheid* era, South Africa has financially gained the maximum benefit in the field of tourism which has rapidly expanded. The number of international airlines with regular flights to South Africa had increased from 23 in 1993 to 59 by the early 1996. Of these, the London route is the most important. British Airways has introduced two flights a day to the Republic. British tourists are the largest visitors to South Africa. British connection is, indeed, important for the Republic's economy, as it is the major investor in South Africa. According to some analysts, political and economic stability/instability in South Africa would directly affect British investments. South Africa seeks British industrial goods, while Britain wants South Africa's agricultural and natural products.[36]

Two state visits, one by the British Queen to South Africa in March 1995 and the other by Nelson Mandela to Britain in July 1996, found warm reception, putting behind the bitter memories of colonialism and *apartheid*. Both visits, according to all press reports, were resounding success. The Queen's visit highlighted the inconsistencies and contradictions in the Commonwealth and Britain's love-hate relationship with South Africa. It brought to the fore South Africa's importance in the Commonwealth. The Commonwealth has some very rich countries, like Britain, Canada, and Australia and some very poor countries like Tanzania, Malawi and Lesotho. In this situation, South Africa can become an instrument for the promotion of North-South dialogue. South Africa, with its First World - Third World personality, could become an important player in the North-South and South-South dialogue.[37]

President Mandela's four-day visit to Britain in July 1996, according to a media commentator, was "the final chapter on *apartheid*". In early 1960, it is interesting how Mandela had managed to enter South Africa. On return to South Africa, he was arrested and sentenced to imprisonment. Some 36 years later, he came to London again, but this time as President of a non-racial South Africa. It was a triumphant return. He showed no bitterness, expressed no criticism of the British government which was not supportive of the sanctions. At a public meeting, Mandela said: "Racism is a blight on the human conscience. The idea that any people can be inferior to another to the point where those who consider themselves to be superior define and treat the rest as sub-human species of humanity even if those who elevate themselves to the status of gods." To those who shared his vision of a new and non-racial South Africa, Mandela said: "We pay tribute to the millions of Britons who, through the years, like others elsewhere in the world, stood up to say 'no' to *apartheid*. Our emancipation is their reward." This speech shows South Africa's attitude towards Britain.

Mandela firmly asserted that the universal struggle against racism and for peace and reconciliation would continue. "We know that the freedom we enjoy is a richly textured gift handcrafted by ordinary folks who would not allow their own dignity as human beings to be insulted, in the acceptance of that gift is contained an undertaking by our people that we shall never again allow our country to play host to racism, nor shall our voices be stilled if we see that another elsewhere in the world is victim of racial tyranny." President Mandela's visit to Britain saw to it that the past differences between the two countries were largely forgotten. He helped in building an understanding with each other. The two countries are, indeed, weaving a web of peaceful and meaningful relationship.[38]

We might say that South Africa's foreign policy is likely to be pro–West in future as much as it is today. This is because of the strong economic ties between the two countries forged over several decades. South Africa is unlikely to take a stance in its foreign policy that would endanger its economic interests. It is likely that in future South Africa would lean more and more on the West in order to vitalize its economy.

The Assessment

The South African foreign policy has been characterized by a lack of direction since the country's first non-racial elections in April 1994. Two issues of the country's place in world politics have been competing for supremacy: the African National Congress's internationalism and the Department of Foreign Affairs' neo-realism. This clash has led to a persistent confusion which specially characterized the debate over the de-recognition of Taiwan and recognition of Communist China. This debate was resolved finally in favour of Beijing in October 1990. Then, there was South Africa's stand on the question of human rights in Nigeria and the execution of Ken Saro-Wiwi. Nigeria was totally isolated on this issue, both within the continent and outside.

It also seems clear that the 'new' South Africa does not have a *new* foreign policy. The formation and conduct of the foreign policy has remained in essence what it was in the era of the minority regime of de Klerk. Apart from occasional rhetorical flourishes, there has been no radical or even distinct ANC input in foreign affairs. The major shifts that occurred were initiated during 1989 - 93, such as the abandonment of military option, and the formal promise of good neighbourliness. They were part of the rationale of the new diplomacy and preceded President Mandela's inauguration by at least three years. It is hardly surprising, therefore, that Alfred Nzo, the Minister of Foreign Affairs of South Africa, has opted for a pragmatic and cautious approach to international issues which, to all intents and purposes, mirrors the approach of his immediate predecessor. After all, a major implicit purpose of the new diplomacy was to tie the hands of a future *post-apartheid* government, particularly regarding South Africa's trading and commercial interests. The conflict that took place between the Department of Foreign Affairs and the ANCs Department of International Affairs during the interregnum has ensured that continuity rather than change has been the dominant characteristic of the new South Africa's international relations.

In particular, the perception of the country's identity and role played by the bureaucrats and formal office-bearers appears to be static. The new South Africa, like the old, still projects itself as a small-to-minimum peripheral power in world politics, while simultaneously assuming unchallenged authority or 'core' status in the regional subsystem. The structural characteristics of the international system, from which these images derive, have not been challenged by the ANC leadership who appears to accept their neo-realist implications for policy: namely, that South Africa is marginalised from, and dependent on, the neo-liberal international political economy, but, at the same time, as the regional superpower it can virtually dictate the terms of subordination to its neighbours. No longer isolated, the Government is now in a position to establish a formal or informal basis, 'the Constellation of States' that was the lynch-pin of the National Party's regional ambitions. Additionally, there has been no conscious effort to create a regional security community. Pretoria's existing military capability means that any discussion of a *post-apartheid* regional order must resolve around the protective framework of a Pax Pretoriana, either tacit or actual, but almost certainly benign.

On the administrative level, the foreign policy of South Africa remains concentrated in the (executive branch of the government) the influence of the legislature is still weak. The tradition of personal diplomacy initiated by Jan Smuts is no longer an exclusively white preserve; the psychological / philosophical conceptual framework, from which policy initiatives emerge, remains in tact. South Africa's traditional strategic culture has not so far been challenged by the new-look formal office-bearers. Foreign policy has been a contested ground in South Africa. Whereas in the past the debate largely centred on the question of legitimacy of the state itself, today it revolves around its overall aims and objectives more especially regarding South Africa-Southern Africa relations - the one area where the government appears to hold the whip hand.

The current controversy related to South Africa's proper regional role and involves three competing scenarios. The first scenarios could be described as the 'do nothing' or 'benign neglect' approach: South Africa's future prosperity lies in forging relations with Europe and Indian Ocean Rim rather than its immediate neighbours. South African leaders argue that since Africa is likely to remain an international basket, the country needs to delink from the continent and become attached to one or the other of the world's great trading blocs. This is expected to have a positive spill-over effect on its neighbours, since they would undoubtedly benefit from a prosperous core, but will be a bi-product of policy, not its central goal. What might be called the ultra-realist view finds some favour in business and industrial circles.

The second approach focuses on the region itself and stresses the need for a quantitative change in South Africa's involvement. It argues for multinational co-operative enterprises in a number of sectors including industry, energy, transport, health, security, agriculture, and assumes that any expansion of trade or contacts will be mutually beneficial for all concerned, it envisages the development of a Southern African Common Market within which Africa would play the hegemonic role. The third approach is by far the most radical because it envisages qualitative change in South Africa-Southern African relations which would involve adopting affirmative action programmes. Its objectives would be to reduce the existing imbalances in order to promote more balanced, long-term, regional development, its proponents argue that this is the only morally correct path in the sense that the new South Africa has a positive duty to look after its long-suffering neighbours, but also the most pragmatic policy since the country's future progress is virtually inextricable from the question as to how well or how poorly they ultimately fare. The central unit of analysis is that in international relations, the state can no longer be taken for granted in Southern Africa. The problem of the regional status can only be resolved on the basis of cooperation and genuine interdependence. Hen ` the argument that the principle task of Pretoria's policy must be to transform regional relations from the current state-centric neo-colonialist base, to non-exploitative approach underpinned by a belief in the doctrine of harmony of interests and egalitarianism.

The Ministry of Foreign Affairs has supported the concept of only limited regional cooperation in the fields of economic and security, and appears content to let the natural asymmetry of power between South Africa and its neighbours produce outcomes. The Government of National Unity (GNU) has formally renounced the military scenario but is conscious of the fact that 'capability' is still an important impulse in foreign policy formulation and conduct because of the country's broad portfolio of available power resources. The primacy of the domestic reconstruction and development programme continues to affect South Africa's conception of its regional role, and proposals for affirmative action, which were a feature of exile politics, appear now to be attractive only to scholar-activists and ideological purists in the universities and trade union movements. By contrast, the ANC leadership seems to have accepted the *increment list* and pragmatic approach to regional development. South Africa's role in world politics is conceived in terms of a fairly narrow conception of the national interests tempered by a cautious commitment to regionalism. Beyond expression of goodwill, the new leaders in reality have not constructed an alternative framework for regional relations. So far most of their external efforts have been directed at building bridges with Western Powers and financial institutions, notably the World Bank (WB) and the International Monetary Fund (IMF).

Clearly, South Africa is an changed state but in terms of its external projection, it still retains much of the habits, norms, values and mind-set of the previous era. Its foreign policy still reflects its domestic needs. Whether or not this augurs well for the future development of the region as a whole remains to be seen. What is certain though is that past patterns of domination will continue to exert themselves well into the late 1990s and beyond. The ANC essentially passive approach to foreign policy issues indicates that the intellectual shift from 'liberal' to 'socialist' to 'neo-conservative' is all but complete, and that it is now unwilling or unable to articulate a programme inVolving radical challenges to the prevailing order. In this sense at least, South Africa really is just a mother-state trying to make ends meet in a fiercely competitive world. The inescapable priority is the quest for domestic reconstruction and economic growth allied to internal political stability. This is likely to work against the more ideological foreign policy postures that were a feature of the ANC's approach to international relations prior to assuming office in 1994.

Another serious problem of South Africa's foreign policy relates to difficulties in interpreting the actions of the South African government. This is not to say that values cannot be identified in the declared foreign policy, but that there is an ambiguity in the application of those values. The dualism in South Africa's foreign policy is the true reflection of what is happening in the country. The amalgamation of the 'old and new' in South Africa took place without the development of new South African values. The principle of universality applied by South Africa to its foreign policy offers a good solution to the problem of values. It is, however, not the ultimate solution because, if values are identified and applied as a basis of foreign policy, the country's national interest will be difficult to identify. This will inevitably mean that when decisions are taken under pressure, clarity and guidance will be found lacking. The contradictions in South Africa's foreign policy are indicative of the lack of values of national interest. The end result is that it is difficult to predict, explain and evaluate South Africa's foreign policy. This holds the danger that the South African government's foreign policy actions will be seen as reactive.

However, on the positive side there have been a number of successes. First, on the organizational side, the Department of Foreign Affairs has displayed an increasing willingness to openly interact with the civil society in the formulation of policy. The publication of the South African Foreign Policy Discussion Document in June 1996, and the subsequent holding of a Foreign Policy Workshop in Johannesburg in September 1996, were illustrative of this new approach. In the same vein, the Department also organized a number of regional workshops and seminars. Secondly, from the late 1996 South Africa has at last shed some of the sensitivity in adopting a less apologetic and more assertive regional / continental role. President Mandela's assumption of the chairmanship of the Southern Africa Development Community at the annual conference in Maseru in August 1996 thrusts the responsibility of redefining the Community's purpose and functions on its regional actor. Now, it has dawned on South Africa's leaders that, if the country is to assume the status of an African power and redress some of the continent's problems, they will have to engage with Africa's problems. This responsibility, even if unsolicited, is undoubtedly the destiny of the continent's major economic and diplomatic power. This diplomacy has set a new standard for the continent.

South Africa has already had a lot on 1 its diplomatic plate since the resumption of normal relations in 1994 in terms of the expansion of bilateral and multilateral ties, the integration or combination of personnel within the Department of Foreign Affairs, and also with respect to the number of policy issues which have sprung from the end of isolation.

In the light of all these considerations, we can say that the South African government's foreign policy is basically sound. There are problems that need to be identified and addressed if South Africa's continued success in global politics is to be assured. Most of the problems relate to internal political developments and the position of the country as an important link between Africa and the rest of the world. There will also be a need for South Africa to always maintain a flexible foreign policy capable of coping with global changes. This will demand careful understanding and monitoring of the continuously shifting international milieu. South Africa will accordingly require are fully defined foreign policy goals and priorities probably with a strong African emphasis.

References

1. S. C. Sacena, Foreign Policy of African Sates (Delhi, Deep and Deep Publications, 1982), p. 9.

2. F. S. Northedge, The Foreign Policy of Powers (London, Faber and Faber, 1968), p. 10.

3. Joseph Frankel, The Making of Foreign Policy: Analysis of Deicision making (London, Oxford University Press, 1963), p. 3.

4. S. C. Saxena, *op. cit.*, p. 12.

5. *Ibid.*, p. 13.

6. *Ibid.*, p. 14.

7. *Ibid.*, p. 17.

8. *Ibid.*, pp. 18-19.

9. *Ibid.*, p. 20.

10. *Ibid.*, pp. 21-22.

11. Nicholas J. Spykman, "Geography and Foreign Policy-I", American Political Science Review (Washington, vol.32 (1) : February 1938, p. 29.

12. Dominic Milazi, "south Africa's Foreign Policy in the Post-Apartheid Ear: What are the Key International Issue", Indian Journal of African Studies (Delhi), vol. VIII (1 & 2) : April and June 1997, p.3.

13. *Ibid.*, pp. 3-4.

14. *Ibid.*, p. 4.

15. Greg Mills, "South Arican's International Relations under Mandela", Indian Journal of African Studies, vol. VIII (1 & 2): April and October 1997, p. 46.

16. Nelson Mandela, "South Africa's future foreign policy", Foreign Affairs (New York), vol. 72 (5) : November-December 1993, p. 87.

17. Greg Mills, *op. cit.*, p. 47.

18. For these and other trade figures, see G. Mills, ed., The South African Year book of International Affairs (Johannesburg, South African Institute of International Affairs, 1996.)

19. Nelson Mandela, *op. cit.*, p. 89.

20. Nata C. Crawford, "South Africa's new foreign and military policy: Opportunities and constraints", Africa Today (Denver), vol. 42 (1-2) : 1995, p. 97.

21. Press Conference by Alfred Nzo, Minister of Foreign Affairs, Cape Town, 21 February 1995, p. 2.

22. Hari Sharan Chhabra, South African Foreign Policy: Principles-Options-Dilemmas (Delhi, Everest Press, 1997), p. 97.

23. Alfred Nozo, *op. cit.*, p. 4.

24. Hari Sharan Chhabra, *op. cit.*, p. 98.

25. *Ibid.*, pp. 98-99.

26. Princeton N. Lyman, South Africa's Promise (Washington, Carnegie Endowment for International Peace, 1996), p. 118.

27. Hari Sharan Chhabra, South African Foreign Policy: Principles-Options-Dilemmas (Delhi, Everest Press, 1997), p. 132.

28. South Africa Yearbook (Pretoria, South African Communication Service, 1995), p.158.

29. Keynote address by Deputy Minister, Aziz Pahad, at the Diamond Jibilee of the Institute of International Affairs, November 1995.

30. Paul-Henry Bischoff, "South African Foreign Policy under a democratic Mandela Government: the growth of an intermediary power", Indian Journal of African Studies (Delhi), vol. VIII (1 & 2): 1997, p. 21.

31. Princeton N. Lyman, *op. cit.*, p. 119.

32. Frederic Chambon, "SA's Foreign Policy worries to allies", The Guardian Weekly (Manchester), 31 March 1996.

33. Princeton N. Lyman, *op. cit.*, p. 119.

34. Hari Sharan Chhabra, *op. cit.*, pp. 123-24.
35. *Ibid.*, p 125.
36. *Ibid.*, pp. 125-27.
37. *Ibid.*, pp. 128-29.
38. *Ibid.*, p. 130.

5

Human Rights and Economic Dimension

Economic federalism has played an important part in the evolution of federalism in the twentieth century as the search for political accommodation between communities divided by history and culture.[1] There are valid reasons for a high degree of regional autonomy in large countries having culturally diverse populations. At the same time, many factors promote the centralisation of power in modern industrial economies. Two contrary impulses are thus apparent. On the one hand, the impetus towards the integration of national economies and on the other the acceptance by democratic governments of a responsibility to assure minimum standards of welfare for all citizens, all seem to call for the enlargement of the powers of national governments. At the same time, a number of countries with strong national governments, democratic pressures have developed for the devolution of economic as well as political power to regions.

South Africa has adopted federal features constitutionally much to be desired in terms of practice and in terms of practical governments.

Historically, South Africa undoubtedly achieved remarkable economic development in the 1960s. For the past 50 years, through the system of apartheid and separate development, economic policies favoured the white minority which resulted in a serious structural weakness in its economy: Equally, these deficiencies created a deep divide between the affluence of a privileged few (mainly whites) alongside the extensive poverty and social deprivation of the majority. A number of big corporate groups, though small in number, captured the major economic sectors like mining and others. In this context, Openheimer and De Beers along with others had enjoyed the apartheid policies by exploiting the South Africa's minerals on the hand and black below on the other. Until the early 1990s, four mining groups controlled 80 per cent of the Johannesburg Stock Exchange, with Anglo-American cooperation and De Beers owning half the value of shares quoted.[2]

South Africa undoubtedly achieved remarkable economic development in 1980, with one of the highest growth rates in the world during that decade. The result of that development, however, was very unevenly distributed, with the 'homelands' (a place for black community) remaining as wretched and overpopulated as ever. Growth in the 1970s was much slower mainly due to international sanctions and partly due to instability of the world economy. The political upheaval resulted into a disturbed political, social and economic situation in South Africa. The Soweto massacre of June 1976, in which hundreds of people died, was a part of these disturbances. These factors had a particularly discouraging effect on foreign investment in South Africa.

The first quarter of 1989 and 1993 showed a drop in the real GDP by 4 per cent resulted the longest recession of the 20th century in South Africa. The most serious manifestation of the recession was the decline in investment, which was equivalent to only 15 per cent of GDP in 1992 recorded well below as compared to earlier levels (24 per cent on average during 1982-85) of GDP since the late 1980s. A low level of investment undermined the economy's future ability to generate growth and adsorb work seekers. Following the establishment of the ANC administration, a major reversal of the flow of investment took place.[3]

More than 100,000 jobs were lost in mining, and over 60,000 in manufacturing in the first half of the 1990s. The Reserve Bank estimated that from the first quarter of 1989 (the beginning of the recession) to the third quarter of 1993, employment in the formal non-agricultural sectors fell by some 410,000. During this period 8 per cent of workers were declared redundant. Unemployment figures continued to rise even with little recovery in the second half of 1993.

A major structural change in the South African economy after the abolition of all forms of influx control (through the Bantustam and homeland policies) resulted into a mass migration to the large towns and metropolitan cities. Disguised unemployment in the rural areas was increasingly registered as overt unemployment in the urban areas. In early 1996 the rate of unemployment increased by only 0.6 per cent, while the labour force grew by 2.5 per cent. Unemployment increased by some 280,000 in that year. A significant two-years wage contract between the Chamber of Mines and the National Union of Mine Workers, which was announced in July 1997, established strict linkages between productivity and wage increase; gold production was to increase by 90 tons in 1997, and this higher level was to be sustained in 1998.[4] If this target was reached the lowest paid, least-skilled workers would receive a 25 per cent rise in wages, which would effectively amount to a minimum wage of R. 1,000 per month for official work and R. 1,150 per month for unofficial work.

In the election in April 1994, the new government acted to address the prevailing negative investor sentiment, with a number of prudent financial and structural policies. These included a programme of progressive fiscal deficit reduction, the constitutional guarantee of the independence of the Reserve Bank, plans for trade liberalization in a number of areas including gold and oil. The government have adopted some measures to redress social imbalances under the RDP and GEAR strategy. The availability of funding to help small and medium sized firms to become established in a number of sectors, from fishing to forestry, to horticulture to manufacturing, the reform of labour legislation to reduce tension in industrial relations, and a commitment to a progressive elimination of capital controls.

By the elections in 1994, there was a consensus that a mixed economy was the appropriate way to develop a strong economy. The focus of the economy was on achieving high rates of growth with economic policies that encouraged the inflow of private foreign investment. A 'letter of intent' was signed with the International Monetary Fund (IMF) in which the government agreed the need to hold the budget deficit in check.[5] An accord was signed by the ANC and the NP giving the Reserve Bank more autonomy, provided that there was 'regular consultation between the governor and the minister of finance'. Although nationalization remains part of the agendas of both COSATU and the SACP, the ANC in government has managed to evade commitment.

View of Different Political Parties on Economic Policies and Human Rights Issue

The left wing parties namely SACP, COSATU which is the part of ANC alliance in national government and PAC, AZAPO and SWAPO (socialist organizations) favour a strong central government and the federal system does not gain any strong advocacy. The ANC has never been strongly in favour of a federal economic issue in South Africa, whereas the DP, NP and the IFP strongly favour the devolution of economic powers between the centre and provinces in South Africa.

African National Congress's (ANC) Economic Policies

When the ANC was unbanned in 1990, it had no economic policy, a peculiar situation for an eight-decade old liberation organization despite the efforts internationally on the left to train a cadre of ANC exile economists. In 1988 Constitutional Guidelines had committed it to a mixed economy. The Freedom Charter of South Africa mentioned some of the features of its economic policies, says: "The people share in the country's wealth, the national wealth of our country, the heritage of all South Africans shall be restored to the people. The mineral wealth beneath the soil, the banks and monopoly industry shall be transferred to the ownership of the people as a whole.

All other industries and trade shall be controlled to assist the well-being of the people; All people shall have equal rights to trade where they choose, to manufacture and to enter all trades, crafts and professions."[6]

The ANC's first serious attempt to fill this lacuna came in the form of a 'Discussion document on economy policy' in 1990 issued by its new department of economic policy (DEP). In its main themes the document echoed policy work done by COSATU's economic trend groups which had been responsible for the most substantial efforts to chart a sustainable and progressive economic strategy. The central theme to the ANC document was the 'restructuring' of the economy which as economist Nicole Nattraas noted, "could include anything from extensive state intervention to conventional market drives structural adjustment."[7]

The ANC's commitment to an export-oriented growth strategy was also ensured, despite warnings from unlikely quarters such as the General Agreement of Tariff and Trade (GATT), that: "export-led growth, while beneficial to the balance of payments, is unlikely to immediately affect levels of unemployment, given the capital intensity of the export-sector, unless labour-intensive downstream industries can be developed.[8] The ANC will speed up the programme to improve the quality of life of the people. The fight against poverty requires a co-ordinated strategy that cuts across all sectors and pays particular attention to rural and disadvantaged areas. The ANC would ensure all programmes work together.

ANC's Housing Policy

Housing is one of the major problems in South Africa. The RDP document assures to provide better houses to low income groups. The first housing minister Joe Slovo, tried hard to implement it in right direction. Even the ANC manifesto 1999 pointed out that:

(1) Seek an honest agreement with the private sector and work with trade unions to channel investments into people's housing.

(2) Focus on developing housing on well-located land, with access to amenities and overcoming the apartheid human settlements patterns based on Group Areas and isolation of the majority from centres of economic activity.

(3) Use other affordable ways of financing houses like micro loans.

(4) Support the peoples Housing process, setting up housing support centres to help poor people build their own houses, share resources and purchase affordable materials.[9]

The ANC remains staunchly committed to the RDP vision that growth and development are thoroughly inter-connected. Without development (like basic needs, creating job, eradicating poverty with education, health, potable water, etc.) growth will mean nothing for the majority of South Africa's people. But without growth, development will not be sustainable.

To ensure both growth and development and to weave them together the ANC is committed to:

> The ANC will continue to expand economic opportunities by speeding up job creation, increasing possibilities for self-employment, entrenching worker rights, advancing work-place equity programmes and developing skill training.
>
> The ANC is committed to progressive taxation, that lightens the tax burden on middle income and poor families and ANC ensured transparent budgeting through detailed medium term budget planning, and continued to give priority to social spending and ensure the resources reach those they are aimed at.

- The ANC will speed up public sector investment through increased capital expenditure and through co-ordinated investment plans of parastatals. The main aim of such investment will be:
- Job creation.
- Increasing the rate of growth of the economy.
- Meeting basic infrastructure needs.
- Promoting development in regions where it is not needed.
- Working together with the private sector to mobilize greater Volumes of investment by private sector.
- Measures to mobilise investment from the private sector.
- Improved education standards for the work-force sector promotion and better telecommunication, transport and other infrastructure.
- Incentives to encourage increased foreign and domestic investment in real, job-creating activities.
- Measures to discourage over-dependence on short-term capital flows and speculative investment.[10]

This is ANC's economic plan. There is little doubt that the economy of South Africa will change and develop over the next decade and this process will have to be recognized by all sections of society.

The Democratic Party and New National Party's Economic Policy

Against a background of mass unemployment, the decision of the National New Party (NNP) government to abandon its policies of previous white minority domination and to seek a negotiated way to a democratic future has profound implications, especially when the constituency of the unemployed far exceeds that of those who presently control the country." Today, both the parties are in favour of privatization. They referred their economic thinking as per guidelines of globalization and market-oriented policies. Moreover, they support a complete liberalization of economic policies which emphasizes only on growth. The development (mainly social one) is the second priority for them. They criticized RDP document, particularly the land redistribution, housing policy, public sector etc. Both the parties are not in favour of strong public sector. After the June 1999 election, both the parties joined together to form a Democratic Alliance. Some of the features of their economic policies highlight their ideas. The core of the New National Party (earlier National Party) job creation policy is:

- Sustainable economic growth in a socially responsible free enterprise economy;
- Flexible labour markets where individuals compete for jobs on the basis of merit, ability and hard work;
- The scrapping of the Employment Equity Act and revising other labour legislation;
- Ending the skewing of the playing field by the Government through the introduction of quotas and other forms of racial discrimination;
- Voluntary membership of trade unions, and the introduction of an ethical code governing the management and leadership of trade unions;
- The promotion of entrepreneurship and the development of the small business sector as a priority:
- Deregulation and the lowering of individual and company taxes;
- The lowering of interest rates, loosening up of exchange control and the reducing of government debt by privatisation;
- Education and career-oriented training, with specific emphasis on young people, women and disadvantaged communities;

Making South Africa a successful competitor in the global economy.[12]

The New National Party believes that the success of housing delivery depends upon:

1. Access to housing for first-time home buyers;
2. The principle of payment for goods and services;
3. Job creation to enable people to have the means to afford housing and maintain their properties;
4. Certainty concerning property rights.
5. Effective and cost-efficient service delivery - Services must be affordable without excessive rates and taxes. Where services can be delivered more cost efficiently by the private sector, then cut wasteful spending.[13]

Both the parties are committed to a non-racial, non-sexist, multiparty democracy that recognises the central role of the family and the community. The principles such as law and order, the rule of law, a free-enterprise economy with social responsibility, federalism and inclusive government from the foundation of our platform.

The Freedom Front's Economic Plan

The FF favours the idea of a 'Volkstaat' an independent white Afrikaner state. It supports total privatization and liberalization of economic policies. Its policies do not reflect the ideas of social development of majority people. It mentioned that RDP is a socialist-oriented document. That is why the FF criticized this document and the issues of the land redistribution, role of public section etc. in particular. Some of the features of its economic policies are:

1. The FF supports a free-market economy. The government must play a limited role in the economy and create and maintain circumstances that offer individuals an equal opportunity to compete in the market.

2. Foreign investments, without which economic growth is not possible, must be promoted by immediately reinstating law and order.

3. Business people and entrepreneurs must be intent upon providing jobs for their own. There must be a central point where employers and jobseekers can meet.

4. Tax income of the state must not exceed 25 per cent of the GDP. Double taxation on retirement funds must be abolished. A person should be taxed during his or her productive working life and retirement benefits should therefore be tax free.[14]

The Inkatha Freedom Party's Economic Views

The IFP resolves to pursue economic growth at all costs and to develop an economy which is liberalised and outside government control. In terms of economic consideration, the IFP constitutional viewpoint provides a mandate for privatization whereas the private sector can provide the same services or product with comparable reliability and efficiency as compared to the government. In addition, the IFP also provides a mandate in respect of the autonomy of the central bank, special parliamentary majorities and requirement of verifiable economic justification for the adoption of a non-balanced budget. The people of South Africa are quite correctly deeply concerned about the present state of the economy, pervasive poverty, rising unemployment, rapidly declining job opportunities and the fact that our money, depreciates daily because of inflation and the deteriorating exchange rate of the Rand against the world's hard currencies.[15]

The United Democratic Movement's Economic Plan

South Africa needs rapid and sustainable socio-economic expansion through enterprise development. The poor performance of the existing macro-economic plan will be addressed in such a way that the positive elements of the plan are enhanced whilst improving the negative aspects. Innovative proposals and specific solution to current shortcoming are the following:

1. The budget deficit, which currently equals 12 per cent of state spending, will be reduced to zero in a 3 year period.

2. A privatization programme, which is beneficial to all South Africans, will be developed.

3. The tax on fuel will be cut to relieve the burden of transport costs on commuters who travel long distances.

4. The tax on personal income, upto R 4000 per month will be abolished.

5. Government programmes which employ and train the unemployed in agricultural and community development projects will be introduced.These programmes will be transformed into self-sustaining, privately owned enterprises, which have the potential to grow, accumulate assets and create employment.

6. The existing 25 per cent levy on all banking transaction will be altered and enhanced to a low ad-valorum rate of 0.05 per cent which should generate additional revenue of at least R 10 billion per annum.

7. A balanced globalization policy will be introduced to rectify the job losses that have occurred as a result of policies that have distorted the South African market.

8. Labour laws will be reviewed to ensure a friendly labour code that will encourage job creation.

9. The housing subsidy should be increased on an annual basis to keep up with the inflation rate. The focus of subsidies should be on building new houses.

10. In order to boost the property market and to make it easier for first-time house-owners to acquire property, transfer duties on all property transactions will be reduced to 1 per cent with full exemption for transaction below R 100,000.

AZAPO's Economic Plan

The AZAPO believes that rampant market forces have failed to ensure the equitable redistribution of wealth and have therefore disqualified themselves as the salvation of the poor. AZAPO is convinced that the phenomenon of globalization has left Africa and the developing countries at the mercy of the world economic forces such as the World Bank and the IMF–AZAPO believes in the centrality of the working class in the struggle for economic emancipation and encourages the establishment of a democratic, independent working class movement. An AZAPO government will reduce the overall tax burden on individuals, especially low and middle income earner. In pursuance of South Africa's wealth redistribution and reform programmes, "we will consider other forms of taxation such as taxation on luxury goods, capital gains tax, property/land tax and others."

The Government's Economic Policies and Its Implementation

More or less, all the political parties favour the policies of liberalization. Some of the parties (mainly ruling groups) emphasize the social development along with the economic growth. The opposition parties concerned on the market and liberalization. The government of South Africa right from the 1994 onwards, adopted different economic policies. These documents reflect the ideology of ANC, SACP, and COSATU on the one hand and the government policies on the other. Some of the policies are:

(1) Macro Economic Research Group (MERG)

MERG was set up in 1991 by the ANC to develop a new macroeconomic model for South Africa. A new economic system would depend on a 'strong private sector interacting with a strong public sector'.[16] If its key proposals were implemented, the MERG model predicted annual growth of 5 per cent in 2004 and the creation of 300,000 new jobs a year. It presented a two phase growth plan (comprising a 'public investment led phase' and a 'sustained growth phase') that tied growth to expanded and efficiently deployed savings and investment. The report saw state investment in social and physical infrastructure (housing, school, education, health services, electrification and road development) in the first phase accounting for more than half of growth and triggering sustained, growth-inducing effects throughout the economy.

The plan represented the most sophisticated popular economy strategy ever devised in South Africa. Yet it was allowed to die an ignominious death soon after the report's release. Making democracy work was savaged in the media and by mainstream economists, responses which some ANC leaders reportedly shared. To be sure, some of its key proposals should be enhanced in COSATU's social equity and job creation document (1993) itself a reactive intervention prompted by the neo-liberal arrogance of the South Africa foundation's Growth for all plan.

On the whole, the perspectives gathered in the MERG report fell victim to a dominant discourse and a balance of forces that had titled inductably at the 1994 COSATU congress mentioned to invoke the examples of low wage Asian economies and tell delegates that "unless we sacrifice, we have determination to tighten our belts ... it is going to be difficult to get our economy to grow.[17]

The interim government of national unity focused on the maintenance of stability and the promotion of economic growth, with initial emphasis laid on a reconstruction and development programme (RDP) which included an undertaking to construct 1 m homes in a period of five years, and to extend basic educational and health facilities to all. The government planned to finance the RDP through savings on security-related expenses and increased revenue resulting from economic growth. Japan and other countries provided sizeable contributions to these programmes.

(2) The Reconstruction and Development Programme (RDP)

The RDP emerged as the most concerted attempt in 1993 yet to devise a set of social, economic and political policies and practices that could transform South Africa into a more just and equal society, Its starting point was an allegedly integrated analysis of South Africa's development crisis of a 'growth plan' that had lost its way and on an awareness that a new path would depend on the achievement of social, political and economic goals.[18] It is more than a development framework aimed at completely reordering politics, the economy and society. The RDP document highlights five sub-programmes: meeting basic needs, developing human resources, building the economy, democratizing the state and implementing the RDP.

The RDP was conceived as an attempt to programme measures aimed as creating a people-centred society which measures progress by the intent to which it has succeeded in securing for each citizen's liberty, prosperity and happiness. It claimed to be an integrated, socio-economic policy. The key to that link would be an infrastructural programme that would provide access to modern and effective services like electricity, water, telecommunications, transport, health, education and training.[19]

Initially the RDP base document had pledged, among other things to:

1. Create 2.5 million new jobs in 10 years;
2. Build one million low-cost homes by the year 2003;
3. Provide electricity to 2.5 million homes by the year 2003, doubling the number of households with such access from the then 36 per cent;
4. Provide running water and sewage system to one million households;
5. Redistribute 30 per cent of agricultural land to small scale black farmers within five years;
6. Shift the health system from curative services towards primary health care, with free medical services for children under six years and pregnant women at state facilities by 1998, all South Africans were to receive their basic nutritional intake, thanks to school-funding and other schemes;

7. Extend infrastructure through a public work programme;

8 Restructure state institutions to reflect the racial class and gender competition of South Africa society.[20]

The implementation of the RDP proved much more difficult than the government had anticipated. However, in early 1996, it was announced that the separate ministry for the RDP was to be abolished, and the programme was transferred to the office of the then Deputy President Thabo Mbeki. The government's schemes to provide housing, electricity and clean water were initially among its most successful services, but unemployment remained very high in the townships. Many communities continued to refuse to pay for services and rents, despite the efforts of the government campaign to persuade them to do so. Moreover the RDP did not achieve its fixed tenure targets. The government came forward with another economic document, which is known as Growth, Employment and Redistribution (GEAR).

The Finance Minister Trevor Manuel immediately declared the Growth, Employment and Redistribution (GEAR) plan 'non-negotiable' in its broad outline, although the government was willing to negotiate the details with their political partners.[21]

The various economists favoured this document and its prescription lit the faces of business leader but shocked many within the ANC alliance. Thabo Mbeki made it clear, "This policy is the central compass which will guide all other sectoral growth and development programmes of the government aimed at achieving the objectives of the RDP."[22]

The document specifically contained only four references to the RDP, except for an annexe which described how the budget deficit target could be met by trimming the RDP fund. According to the National Institute for Economic Policy (NIEP), GEAR represents a recourse to the policy goals and instruments of the post apartheid regime, a harsh but plausible judgment.[23]

GEAR promised to increase annual growth by an average of 4.2 per cent, create 1.35 million new jobs by the year 2000, boost exports by an average 8.4 per cent per annum through an array of supply-side measures, and drastically improve social infrastructure.

The rancour that greeted GEAR stemmed from the methods choosen to achieve these targets. The plan hinged fundamentally on an inplausibly massive increase in private sector investment. This would be elicited by:

- Slashing trade spending to drive the budget deficit down to 3 per cent of GDP by the year 2000;
- Keeping inflation in single digits;
- Reducing corporate taxes and providing tax holidays for certain investments;
- Gradually phasing out completely exchange control regulations;
- Encouraging wage restraint by organized workers;
- Creating a more 'flexible' labour market, possibly by deregulating certain categories of unskilled work and exempting small business from aspects of the new labour regime, and
- Speeded-up privatization.

GEAR's growth projections hinged on increases in private investment and net non-gold exports, as well as substantial state expenditure in social infrastructure. The strategy unloaded the duty of economic salvation squarely onto the shoulders of the private sector not only as the source of private investment but through partnerships in the public sectors. The government justified its privatization programme in several ways – as a way to 'facilitate economic growth', 'find the RDP', 'create wider ownership in the South African economy', 'mobilize private sector capital', 'reduce state debt', 'enhance competitiveness of state enterprises', 'promote fair competition' and 'finance growth and requirements for competition'.[24]

The experience of 'jobless growth' from 1994 to 1996 brought home the realization that economic growth does not necessarily cause unemployment. GEAR therefore presented specific job creation targets. It predicted 1.35 million new jobs by 2000, of which 833,000 would be created through GEAR adjustments, 308,000 through higher economic growth, 325,000 through 'changes in the flexibility of labour market' and 200,000 through 'government-included employment'.

Politically, this was GEAR's Achillies' heels, for the prickly notion of labour market flexibility was central to this aspect of the plan. In finance minister Trevor Manuel's words: "As South Africa proceeds with trade liberalisation and adapts to international competition, downward pressures will be placed on unskilled wages. If this is not accommodated by the labour market, then unemployment will rise."[25]

The assumptions embedded in GEAR's call for 'regulated flexibility' demand scrutiny. Job creation stood at the centre of GEAR's efforts to alleviate poverty. Its premise, however, was that employment levels are determined largely by the real wage rate. The economy is already characterised by considerable wage flexibility, with wages in certain industries fluctuating dramatically. The ILO has found that in sectors such as metal goods, footwear, paper products, furniture and plastics, average black wages relative to subsistence actually fall between 1984 and 1992. Secondly, the truism that rising black wages have encouraged capital intensive production, thereby depressing private sector employment,[26] has been soundly debunked, leading the ILO to conclude 'that the available studies have not demonstrated either that real wages have been rigid or that they have had a strong negative effect on employment. Thirdly, while employment creation is one way of reducing poverty and social inequality, it does not necessarily have this effect in employment creation occurs mostly in low wage jobs.[27]

Finally, GEAR recognised the need to improve labour productivity, but focussed on training as the remedy, at the risk of downplaying the example of other factors that cause low productivity – low capital and managerial productivity, low wages and the apartheid wage gap, poor management and the under-utilization of production capacity.

Trade, Taxes and Financial Implications

GEAR's other main features require brief mention. The strategy correctly assumed a continued drop in the share of foreign revenue provided by gold exports. Thus it aimed to boost manufactured exports and trigger a staggering 23 per cent increase in the export and GDP ratio within four years. NIEP regard this target as 'unrealistic and unattainable', particularly because 'the government has not developed a carefully formulated and precisely targeted industrial strategy good to those sub-sectors that have potential for export growth'. Yet GEAR provided no detailed linkage between its macroeconomic adjustment and industrial policy. Furthermore, growth in export GDP ratio registered by other countries prompt scepticism about GEAR's 23 per cent target.

The abandonment of financial controls effectively renders a strategy like GEAR hostage to the vagaries of finance capital. By allowing the uncontrolled penetration of domestic financial markets by foreign capital and encouraging the migration of local capital, patterns of investment are swept out of the ambit of government policy. In almost all cases, the financial system of these countries have been tightly controlled and have operated in ways very different from the free regime.

GEAR's restructuring of taxes was manifestly non-progressive. In 1996, 37 per cent of tax revenue was derived from indirect taxation and other taxes. Several options existed to achieve greater progressiveness, including a capital gain tax., a tax on luxury consumption and a tax on unproductive land. Reportedly, a tax on capital equipment was mooted, but rejected. Instead, personal and corporate taxes were to be reduced if growth occurs, and tax holidays would be offered for selected investments. Overall revenue was slated to increase by way of more effective tax collection.

The Assessment

The different economic policies and the implementation of it can be observed in the budget. The budget sets ambitious goals for continuing the transformation of South African society. More than 60 per cent of expenditure goes to social services, including health, welfare and housing. The 1998 budget receives a healthy increase from 20.2 billion to 25.1 billion, which was an increase of 25 per cent. By 2000-2001, this figure will increase to R 28.1 billion, includes allocation for a hospital rehabilitation programme. Expenditure on welfare services and social grants will increase to R 19.8 billion from R 18.4 billion in 1993-99 to R 22.2 billion in 2000-2001. Education gets a huge R 5 billion increase to R 45 billion which will further increase to over R 50 billion by 2000-2001, proving the government's commitment to human resource development. Along with it, the land redistribution gets R 685 million increasing to R 967 by the end of the three year cycle.

The budget provides a tax relief mainly to middle class people. The 1999 budget reduces R 3.7 billion tax proves the government's commitment to lowering personal taxes.

To sum up, it is rightly remarked that South Africa need growth and distribution. All the political parties more or less are agreed on these policies. It is true that the economic federalism is the right direction for the development of South Africa. The support of all the major parties will strengthen the process of federalism on the one hand, and build a new society on the other.

References

1. Azil Mazoomdar, "The Political economy of modern federation" ed by Balveer Arora and Dougles V. Vermay in *Multiple Identies in a single state* (Konard Publishers, Delhi (India, 1995), p. 197.

2. Heather Deegan, *South Africa Reborn: Building a vow democracy* (London, UCL Press, 1999), p. 127.

3. South of Sahara, 1999, p. 990.

4. *Ibid.*, p. 991.

5. *Overseas Development Institute* (1994, Political liberation and economic reform, London 001), p. 40.

6. Anthony W. Maru, *Lessons of struggle : South African Internal opposition, 1960-1990* (Cape Town, Oxford University Press, 1992), p. 245.

7. P. Bond, "An International Perspective on the people-driven character of the RDP", *African Communist* (Johannesburg), Vol. 144, 2nd quarter, 1996, p. 8.

8. African National Congress Manifesto (Marshaltwon, 1999), p. 18.

9. *Ibid.*, p. 20.

10. I.W. Stadler, "Political economic of post apartheid South Africa", ed. by Alexander, Johansten in *Constitution making in the South Africa* (London, Leicestor University Press, 1993), p. 144.

11. New National Party Manifesto, 1999, p. 13.

12. The Freedom Front Party Manifesto, 1999, p. 6.

13. National Council Resolution, 29 April 2000, p. 399.

14. Heori Moris, *South Africa : Limits to change, the Political Economy of Transition* (London, Zed Books, 1998), p. 101.

15. *Ibid*, p. 103.

16. B. Freund, "The RDP: Half Full?" *Southern Africa Report* (Torento), Vol. 9, No. 5, July 1994.

17. A. Shepard, "The Task Ahead", *Africa Report* (New York), July/ August 1994, pp. 38-41.

18. M. Kentridge, "The Economic Debate in South Africa", *Development Update*" (Johannesburg), Vol. 7, 1993, p. 6.

19. S. Geb, ed., *South Africa's Economic Crisis, Capetown* (David Philip & Zed Books, 1991), pp. 29-30.

20. Hein Marais, *op. cit.*, p. 16.

21. NIEP (National Institute for Economic Policy), 1996, Making the RDP work : Draft submission for the RDP white paper, NIEP, Johannesburg, p. 2.

22. Hein Marias, *op. cit.*, p. 163.

23. *Sunday Time* (Pretoria), 23rd June 1996, p. 468.

24. P. Fallan, ed. "South Africa : Economic Performance and Policies : Informal Discussion papers on Aspects of the Economy of South Africa X10.7, World Bank, Washington, 1994.

25. E. Hobsboom, *Age of Extremes : The short twentieth century* (London, Abacus Press, 1995), p. 534.

26. J. Ghosh, 1997, "India's structural adjustment : An Assessment in Comparative Asian Content" (Seminar paper), Jawaharlal Nehru University, New Delhi, p. 17.

27. NIEP, *op. cit* p. 9.

6

Human Rights and Social Dimension

One of the most important issues discussed recently is the role played by civil society in promoting and sustaining liberal democracy. One central feature of a functioning democracy presented in the classic study by Almond and Verba in 1963 was the establishment of a supportive 'civic culture'.[1] The intention of Almond and Verba's study was to examine the extent to which a pattern of political attitudes and an underlying set of social attitudes was supportive of a stable democratic process. The cleavage within society would be managed and balanced by a civic culture that combined levels of citizen activity with passivity, tradition with modernity, political parties, interest groups, Voluntary associations and neutral media, which would contribute to a 'pluralistic culture' based on communication and persuasion, a culture of consensus and diversity, a culture that permitted change but moderated it.[2]

In the early 1990s, South African anti-apartheid intellectuals and activists came forward in favour of the idea of civil society. Like many others fighting for democratization around the world over the last one decade and so these intellectuals need a society based on democracy.

Democracy is the process by which a multi-cultural society (minority and the majority people) can achieve fundamental rights based on equality and fraternity. A civil society is a kind of empty public space, protected by formal state guarantees of individual liberty and social order and open to multiple races by free and equal citizens. The debate about civil society in the South African anti-apartheid camp has been carried out in two principal areas of the labour movement and the white movement. Here the transitional constitutional phase that began in 1990 stimulated an extended exchange about the possibility of a democratically and socially transformative version of corporation in the 'new South Africa'.[3] The civic movement in the townships during the early 1990s began to articulate the demand for a rigorous and autonomous civil society in which civic associations could play a prominent role. Civil society is also seen as a way of 'securing substantive potential rights and freedoms, essential for a functioning democracy' in an arena outside of state.

South Africa's civics in theory represented a cross class coalition of 'Collective Consumers' straddling the whole of urban space, at least outside white residential areas. It was the extended character of this township constituency, and the absence until 1995 of legitimate municipal government to represent it politically which gave credence to the civic claim to represent 'communities' or civil society. Under the United Democratic Front (UDF), a movement was launched to organize and lead popular opposition to the tricameral parliament. The UDF operated a number of groups like multiracial confederation of affiliated labour, church, student and civic organisations in support of civic society.[4]

The UDF affiliated organizations tended to move towards a national civic federation, which became the South African National Civic Organization (SANCO). SANCO has its roots in the radical civics formed as part of the township resistance movement of the 1980s. These civic groups organized themselves around local basic issues such as rent and township services. Recently SANCO has found itself to be at a crossroads. W.M. Gunede argues, "The accelerating pace of political change since South Africa's first democratic elections in April 1994 have forced the whole spectrum of civil society organizations to redefine their roles."[5] Non-Governmental organizations are one element of civil society. They are non-profit making groups organized by communities or individuals to respond to basic needs that are not being met by either government or the market.[6]

The Development Resource Centre estimates that South Africa has around 54,000 NGOs operating in areas ranging from non-formal education to community development projects, to feeding schemes, to medical and scientific research institutes. A total of 20,000 of the 54,000 NGOs are development in character, which includes some 2000 civic organizations, 9000 educational agencies, 1000 organizations which provide finances and services to grass root groups and 10,000 other community-based associations of various types. This financial support during the apartheid era was seen crucial to the development of community activities solidarity and opposition to government policies and actions.

A European policy document stated that future funding would be based on strict criteria; projects should take into account of regional and national policy; they should seek to address poverty and the marginalization of sections of the population through discrimination and they should make efficient use of financial, human and other available resources.

It is inevitable that NGOs need to reconsider their roles. South Africa's new government is accountable to its citizens for the first time in the country's history and of necessity needs to play a more active role in delivering services to the population. Albic Sachs believes that for NGOs to operate as a vibrant sector and to contribute to solving national problems, attention must be paid to five objectives:

1. The right to these bodies to exist and function actively with the requisite degree of autonomy;

2. Their right to co-operate with each other and with the government to achieve the objectives of the constitution;
3. The right to receive backing or benefits when undertaking certain activities that promote the national interest;
4. The right not to be co-opted or muzzled when co-operating with the government;
5. The right to be consulted and to be involved in the process of elaborating new legislation which touches their areas of interest and to monitor the laws and ensure that they are applied in a just and effective manner.[7]

However, a close funding relationship between the government and NGOs rather undermines civil society supposedly operating in the space between government and society.

Civil Society Democracy

A powerful new perspective developing in South Africa concern the need to nurture what is called 'civil society'. This term of 'civil society' usually refers to 'associational activity outside the state' and civil society thereby represents a commitment to democratic participation above and beyond the official forms of representative government. Civil society express a scepticism toward the statist politics which has dominated in independent African states. There is a tendency in civil society thereby to assume that all things in civil society are good and all things in the state are bad.[8]

This civil society in South Africa has emerged institutions with strong democratic commitments. There are tensions inherent in both the liberal and radical definitions of civil society between citizen autonomy and state coercion. Citizens are moving freely in the state, yet subject to its laws. The state both enlarges and circumscribes freedom, it may abridge some liberties. Liberal and radical descriptions of civil society provide no warrant for search, seizure or incarceration, torture and capital or corporal punishment. On the other hand, both liberals and radical would deny citizens the freedom of assault, injure or kill other citizens, to seize property from them without legal sanctions, or to threaten or incite such actions. There are additional liberties which the state can abridge on the radical definitions; those arising from forms of ownership which violate the democratic rights of workers contribute to systematic and cumulates social inequality. The formalising of right and duties offers citizens some reassurance against arbitrary power and unfair treatment. While providing no guarantees against the determined abuse of law, constitutional and legal protections offer a symbolic recourse to citizens claiming entitlements or seeking redress against injustices.

The kinds of rights which are most suited to a civil society of free equals are those invested in citizens. There are no rights attaching to groups which do not attack of each of their members, and there are no rights which members of one group can claim that members of another groups can deny.

The normatively ideal society is understood in South Africa is compatible with and may require a radical redistribution of wealth and a rough equalisation of income. A civil society underpinned by citizens rights has another characteristic which complicates the vision of a socialist civil society. While a rights-protected civil realm is likely to yield democratic benefits, these are not automatic or guaranteed. Civil society itself possesses no shared purpose or end. If individual rights include the freedom of expression association and self-narration, then individuals are entitled in principle to define their own ends.

The state democracy that best supports the civil society defended here in above all procedural. It codifies the rules of political competition and supplies the institutional field upon which that competition proceeds, it is not itself biased towards a particular party or substantive ideology. Like civil society itself, it has no inherent purpose other than to facilitate the purpose of free and equal citizens. While democratic game rules are procedural, particular parties and the governments in power legitimately pursue substantive ends and programmes. A decision about whether democratic rules apply to the economic enterprise is not neutral, it may take a position in between capitalism and socialism. There are various factors which directly influence implementation of those policies, check the right to private property and limited its jurisdiction. As far as possible, though the ideological content and direction of state politics must be determined in the field of free and unrigged democratic competition. It is not the business of a democratic constitution to ordain ends or substitute itself for politics. It is more visible in the multiplural society like South Africa.

Ethnicity and Human Rights

The South African political system is characterized by cultural diversity, communal conflict and the domination of a black majority by a white minority. This situation in itself does not make the system unique or even unusual. However, what does make it exceptional is the way in which a dominant majority rules the subordinate majority, through the policy of "apartheid" or "separate development" which provided for a system of enforced separation between three racially defined population, categories - 'Whites', 'coloured' and 'black.'[9] The basic building block of the policy of apartheid and the legal measure which formally compelled racial and ethnic 'group membership' was provided by Population Registration Act, which subdivided the South African population into three "population groups" - whites, blacks and coloureds. The classification was done in terms of the definition of a white person, who according to the Act, is a person who an ethnic group consists of people who are conscious of themselves as being of a kind. They are united by emotional bonds and concerned with the perservation of their type.[10]

The policy of apartheid involves the separate and differential treatment of three population categories in virtually all spheres of life. The Prohibition of Mixed Marriages Act and Immorality Act, now repealed, were aimed at preventing any further biological integration of the white population category and any of the other categories. The Group Areas Act and the Reservation of Separate

Amenities Act are the most important laws limiting social contact between population categories, white political separation is achieved through the Separate Representation of Votes Act, the Promotion of Bantu Self Government Act, the Prohibition of Political manifestation of these laws have included the establishment of separate residential areas, separate educational facilities, and separate in public transport, public amenities and public health facilities. In the political sphere they had brought representative institutions in a wide variety of political sub-systems. In 1980, political powers at central government level had been monopolized by whites, who had the exclusive right to vote for representation in Parliament - the sovereign legislature. The Tricameral Parliament of 1983 made provision for a separate chamber for elected representatives of the white population category, the Indian sub-category within the coloured population and the majority black population remain excluded.[11]

During the constitutional negotiations (mainly in CODESA) these interests have responded to democratization by using ethnic identity to defend old privileges. The post 1990 South Africa faced real crisis in dealing with the ethnic question. This phased witnessed violence (among different groups), demand of an independent Afrikaner state, status of traditional leaders, language rights and demand for independent Kwa Zulu state.

Ethnicity vs. Democracy

This is an important issue, particularly in South Africa. Ethnicity has been the basis on which political demands have been made. The ANC, PAC and SACP had negotiated a transition with the interest groups of white homeland parties and other ethnic leaders. The 1996 constitution of South Africa has taken care of various regional and group interests. For many scholars, ethnicity constitutes a fundamental problem for democratization, one that must be accommodated if there is to be genuine representation and stability. South Africa is a plural society in which a number of cultural and ethnic interests need to be accommodated without the fear of domination by other such groups. The Bill of Rights has provided such an opportunity so that the interests of each group may not ignored. Chapter one of the new Constitution has recognised these interests. The Constitution says, under section 6(1), "The official languages of the Republic are Sepedi, Sesotho, Setzwana, Siswati, Tishivenda, Xitsonga, Afrikaners, English, isi Ndebele, isi Xhosa and isi Zulu and in section 6(4)." The national government and provincial governments by legislature and other measures must regulate and monitor their use of official languages. Without detracting from the provisions of subsection (2), all official languages must enjoy partly of esteems and must be treated equitably."[12]

1. A pan South African language Board established by national legislation must

(a) Promote, and create conditions for the development and use of

  (i) all official languages

  (ii) the Khai, Nama and San languages and

  (iii) Sign language, and

(b) Promote and ensure respect for

  (i) all languages commonly used by communities in South Africa, including German, Greek, Gujarati, Hindi, Portuguese, Tamil, Telegu and Urdu and

  (ii) Arabic, Hebrew, Sanskrit and other languages used for religious purposes in South Africa.[13]

Religion

The Constitution of 1997 describes South Africa as a democratic state founded on the values of human dignity, equality, non-racialism and non-sexcism. A bill of rights affirms a broad set of individual and social rights. Still controversial sections on the freedom of religion and on the rights of cultural, religious and linguistic communities. They allow for religious observances at state aided institution for legislation recognizing marriages and other practices according to different religious system of personal and family law, and also for specific communities to maintain their own associations. Apartheid prevented the country from falling the problem of poverty and the gap between rich and poor has widened. Most religious communities support the government Reconstruction and Development Programme, which attempts to meet the basic needs of the poor abolish discrimination, redress policies of exploitation and repression and reserve economic distortions.[14]

Other Social Changes and Question of Human Rights

1. Land Issues

According to apartheid policies on the division of land in South Africa, roughly 13 per cent of the land was originally legally earmarked for Black occupation. The other 87 per cent of the land was allocated to mainly whites. In 1991, when state President de Klerk scrapped all the so-called "Pillars of apartheid", the statutory basis for racial ownership of Land in South Africa was abolished Racial ownership was effected through the Land Act of 1913, the Black Trust and hand Consolidation Act of 1936 and the Group Areas Act of 1950. The Population Registration Act was also scrapped. With the statutory impediments now removed the spatial patterns of racial ownership of land still remains as some of the most unequal legacies of the past. And this refers mainly to rural, and not urban land. The problem of unequal access to land ownerships is one of the major issues confronting post-apartheid reconstruction and structural adjustments in South Africa. It is also a key issue in the reconciliation debate, especially for those blacks who were forcibly removed from tribal colour who was removed for the sake of group areas policies. For the PAC, normally associated with the so-called "black left", the issue of land reform is the most urgent political problem to be settle in South Africa today.

Its prescriptions are clear—all private ownership of land in South Africa dating back to 1682 - should be terminated as the state should assume ownership of all land, white and black farmers should continue to remain the backbone of agriculture but, their land rights should be vested in occupation and lease rights only, white the seize of farming units should be limited by legislation and finally, large portions of white owned land, especially in the rural areas, should be redistributed to blacks, but without any compensation. This is the most radical view on land rights, and according to opinion polls the PAC enjoys less than 5 per cent of public support in South Africa.

Land Redistribution

Land redistribution will be a crucial question for the incoming majority government in South Africa during the first election. Cyril Ramphasa, secretary-general of the African National Congress, is probably not overstating the problem in this line from a recent speech on land reform : "unless we settle the land question, we do have a country. If we handle it badly, we tear South Africa into pieces. If we manage it well, we create the foundation of a truly united nations.[1,15] Millions more are simply in need of land for settlement, whether urban or rural. In the former homelands, 83 per cent of black households are estimated to fall below the poverty line, largely the result of land shortage. It is a massive problem.

Mr. Derek Honekom, the newly-appointed minister of land affairs, from the African National Congress says, "If you don't have a land reform programme with some significant effect it comes back repeatedly to haunt you. People's grievances don't first vanish."[16] He points out that land reform is central to the Reconstruction and Development Programme which calls for 30 per cent of South Africa's land to be redistributed over five years beginning next years. The commission on restitution of land rights and a land claims court setup to deal with the claims of forced land removal victims.[17]

Original land may be returned to them or, where this is not feasible, alternative state-owned land or other compensation will be provided. But under the Bill of Rights, the interests of existing as well as original land owners must be respected. The Constitution bars appropriation except for 'public purposes' and requires that just and equitable compensation be paid, taking into account factors such as market value use of the property and value of investment in it. Rural restructuring and restitution oxtails more than first the acquisition of last land, says, Mr. Hankom, "Good planning, the settlement of people, the provision of infrastructure and services, economic support programmes, suitable development and very importantly, community institution building are essential elements of the programme. Mr. Hankom does not mention reform of agricultural markets - the ministry of agricultural is the responsibility of opposition National Party - but the governments programme includes measures to stimulate competition in agricultural markets and reduce barriers to entry, as an essential adjust to land reform. According to Sremano, "there are three legs to the land reforms process in South Africa. They are restitution, which is the responsibility of the commission redistribution and reform of land tenure. The last two are the responsibility of the ministry of land affairs for South Africa."[18]

Land is a very emotional and Volatile issue in South Africa Everyone is so passionate about the land. This energy can be used to drive along the process of restitution, therefore reconciliation and justice. People can be brought together by their connection to the earth. Any approach to the resolution of the land issue must be sensitive to and respect people spiritual connection to Mother Earth.

(2) Housing Problem

Alongwith the land issue, housing is the another burning issue in South Africa. African National Congress has promised to build at least low cost houses in five years. Apart from setting this ambitious target, assisted by a R-12.5 million state subsidy, the party also vowed to 'transform' and upgrade the migrant workers hostels which house Inn residents and bring electricity to atleast 2.5 m houses by the year 2000. The housing backlog cannot be left to the market, argues the minister`private sector representatives one unanimous that the market requires the assistance and intervention direct and indirect of the state. Deliberate neglect of black urban housing-apartheid's architects treated black South Africans as only temporary residents in white cities - created a backlog of between 1.5 m and 2 m homes. Even if government sought only to keep up with the annual demand caused by population growth, it could face a formidable tasks, about 240,000 new homes each years need to be built.

In the Pretoria-Witswatersrand Veruning (PWV) province done, 1 million people need decent housing some 200,000 people have in recent years established squatter settlements, driven to the region in search of work or to escape from the apartheid laws restricting movement. Capital Subsidy Scheme (CSS) was lanuched in March 1991 by the state financed independent Development Trust, established a year earlier to managed discourse a R-2000 m fund "to enhance the standard of living of disadvantaged communities." The R 750 m scheme offered 113,000 subsidies of R 7,5000 in 103 projects around South Africa.[19]

Obligibility was invited to household earning less than R 1,000 a month and giving registered ownership of a rerviced site. There would be provided with water and waterborne sanitation, access by graded road to earth, site, and paved bus routes. On completion, the project will have provided facilities for between 5 and 10 per cent of the law income population need houses. The assessment needs to be put in the content of the trouble times. Housing was in the political arena, with efforts to tackle the problem set back by political violence, rent boycott and tension created by the economic recession and rising unemployment. But as the assessment goes into more detail it becomes clear that for all its achievement there are serious problem which current housing strategy has to take into account. The government can go a long way towards meeting there expectations says Mr. Slovo, with a programme in which government subsidies will be accompanied by private sector participation. A forthcoming white paper will propose :

1. Provision of a maximum grant of R 12,500 for those earning less than R 1,500 9 months.
2. Consumer protection : measures to prevent speculation and ensuring quality control.
3. Provision of state-owned land for low cost housing.

The Truth and Reconciliation Commission (TRC)

Reconciliation is about making amends. In the South African historical context it was assumed that reconciliation would mean making amends for the social, political and economic injustices that were committed against the black masses, by the ruling white elite, their corporate founders and tl eir constituency institutionalised injustices that were founded on race, creed and sere. It was called Apartheid, but it was much worse than simple racial apartness.[20] Reconciliation is not about forgetting what happened in the past. Nor can it be achieved if we lack understanding of the motivations and the rationale that inspired there injustices.

The parliament in 1995 approved the establishment of a truth and reconciliation commission (TRC) and 17 members were appointed to the commission by Nelson Mandela. Desmond Tutu become chairman of the TRC. The commission began by conducting public hearings throughout the country, at which former victims of human rights violations gave evidence. From August 1996 the TRC heard representations from political parties. Although de Klerk formally apologized for the policy of apartheid, he denied that he or other members of the previous government had ordered to condoned illegal activities.

Views of National Party and Democratic Party

The NP and DP want to let bygones begones. They want to ignore the fact of social and economic legacies of the apartheid will be for many years to come. The past still lives in our communities. Most black people still live in abject poverty caused by decades of unjust impoverishment. This, while whites still reap the fruits of 46 years of deliberate unjust enrichment.

The NP reluctantly offers qualified apologies that some only to embarrass themselves and anger their victims. It confesses half truth and then experts reconciliation. It selectively forgets the worst evils it committed against the masses. It never tell us how it strategically emptied the offers of our country in a bid to sink the economy - and today it refuses to contribute to the revival of the economy. It blames Apartheid crimes on individuals who are either dead or dying. The NP must learn the reconciliation does not reflect weakness, but strength. In its weakness it admits that it does not have anything to offer.[20]

The Difference Between the ANC and NP

- The NP perfected Apartheid and used religion to justify it. The ANC fought Apartheid tooth and nail was justified by universal morality. Yet the ANC was more than willing to testify before the TRC, while the NP shied away from it.
- The NP, imprinted the unfounded notion of 'swart gavaar' on the minds of white South Africans - the ANC dared to challenge and eradicate that fear.
- The NP forced white youths to fight Apartheid wars through forced conscription. Many died or were mutilated - the ANC called on all the youth of the country to join in the campaign for a new and reconciled South Africa.[21]
- The NP feels enough has been given to blacks in their quest for equality now that everyone has the right to vote, associate and socialise without fear.
- The ANC knows there is no freedom without economic emancipation, through redistribution, through the

opening up of access to economic activity to black and through affirmative action.

- The NP wants us to believe that the past belongs to the past, but it knows that we are still infested with the cancer of racism - a cancer that can only be treated with the healing powers of national reconciliation.
- The NP believes we can only go forward by keeping the near view mirror misted. The ANC stresses that advancing the new nation is only possible through open, honest and full disclosure.

Views of Inkatha Freedom Party (IFP)

Inkatha Freedom Party supports the social issues, which was raised by ANC in RDP documents. Earlier, there was no clearcut stand of IFP on land redistribution. The reason behind it that they like to protect the rights to traditional tribal leaders on land. The Department of land affairs has justified their demand. The process of redistribution starts after a lengthy scientific investigation. Alongwith it, IFP supports for better education, health, employment, housing and other issues. IFP is more keen to protect the rights of traditional leaders. They demand for a special status to be given in the constitution. The ANC recognises the status of traditional leaders and very soon they are going to announce the modelities regarding the status and powers of traditional leaders with in the federal government."[22]

Assessment

The growth of civic society needs a comprehensive form of government. It is only possible in a democratic set up where the need of civic culture and society is considered an essential part of it. The civic culture needs a strong economy through which it can provide that maximum facilities of bread, cloth and house (shelter). South Africa initiate the process of change in the society. This change may balance the gap of black, white and coloureds. The existing inequality interns of basic fulfilled through strong economic policies. There policies can help the common mass by providing them employment opportunities, better education, health and other which can be discussed in the subsequent chapter.

References

1. G.A. Almond and S. Verba, *The Civic Culture* (Princeton, Princeton University Press, 1963), p. 35.

2. Heather Deegan, "Civil society citizenship and identity" in South *Africa Reborn : Building a new Democracy* (London, UCL, Press, 1999), p. 65.

3. R. Mattes, Gilomee and James, L. Schlemmer, "The elections in the western cape'", in *Launching democracy in South Africa* (New Heven, Yale University Press, 1996), p. 121.

4. M. Bratton, J. Harbesan D. Rothchilld (eds.), "Civil Society and Political transitions" in *Civil society and state in Africa* (Boulder, Lynne Lienner, 1994), pp. 55-56.

5. W.M. Huoncde, Civics at the cross roads Democracy in Actioı. (10) 5, Van Gunstrormy 1978, Notes on a theory of citizenship. In *democracy, consensus and social contract* (Loıdon, Sage Press, 1996), p. 240.

6. D. Williams and T. Young, *Civil Society and Democratisation* (Warwick, British International Studies Association, 1993), p. 251.

7. Review of African Political Economy, "Ethnicity Society and Conflict in Natal, ROAPE Publication Ltd., 1994.

8. Pierre bu Tait and Francies Theron, "Ethnic and Minority Groups, and Constitutional change in South Africa", *Journal of Contemporary African Studies* ( ), Vol. 7, No. 1/2, April 1998, pp. 133-147.

9. *Ibid*, p. 136.

10. Blade Mzimande, "The Zulu kingdom Buthelezi short cut to power", *The African Communist* (South Africa) first quarter, 1994, p. 13.

11. *The Constitution of South Africa*, Government Publications, 1996, p. 98.

12. *Ibid.* p. I5.

13. *The Encyclopedia of Politics and Religion*, Robert Wuthnow, Vol. II (United Kingdom of Routledge), London, 1998, p. 237.

14. Simon Bekker, *Ethnicity in focus, the South African Case* (Durban Indicator South Africa, 1993), pp. 6-15.

15. M. Mayekiso, '"Institution that themselves need to be watched over", *Urban Forum*. Vol. 4, No. (l) (1993), p. 37.

16. R. Simbuton, *Ethnic stratification -A Comparative Approach* (New York, Macmillan, 1965), p. 40.

17. Daryle Glraser, "South Africa and the limits of civil society", *Journal of Southern African Studies* (glaslgrow), Vol. 23, No. (1), March 1997, p. 127.

18. Heather Deegan, *op. cit.*,p. 150.

19. Gerhard Mare, *Ethnicity and Politics in South Africa* (London, Zed Press, 1993), pp. 72-73.

20. Survey on South Africa, Voter's Crucial Yardstick Michael Hatman Reports on Housing expectation, 1999, p. 3.

21. *Ibid.*, p. 6.

22. Oh. Hyden, "Rethinking theories of the state", *Africa Insight* (Pritoria), No. 26, Vol. 1, 1996, p. 65.

7

The Constitution of Republic of New South Africa 1994 : Bill of Rights

We, the people of South Africa,

Recognise the injustices of our past:

Honour those who suffered for justice and freedom in our land:

Respect those who have worked to build and develop our country; and

Believe that South Africa belongs to all who live in it, united in our diversity.

We therefore, through our freely elected representatives, adopt this Constitution as the supreme law of the Republic so as to –

Heal the divisions of the past and establish a society based on democratic values, social justice and fundamental human rights;

Lay the foundations for a democratic and open society in which government is based on the will of the people and every citizen is equally protected by law;

Improve the quality of life of all citizens and free the potential of each person; and

Build a united and democratic South Africa able to take its rightful place as a sovereign state in the family of nations.

May God protect our people.

Nkosi Sikelel iAfrika. Morena boloka setjhaba sa heso.

God seen Suid-Afrika. God bless South Africa.

Mudzimu fhatutshedza Afurika. Hosi katekisa Afrika.

Republic of South Africa

1. The Republic of South Africa is one sovereign democratic state founded on the following values

   (a) Human dignity the achievement of equality and the advancement of human rights and freedoms.

   (b) Non-racialism and non-sexism

   (c) Supremacy of the constitution and the rule of law

   (d) Universal adult suffrage, a national common voters roll, regular elections and a multi-party system of democratic government to ensure accountability responsiveness and openness.

Supremacy of Constitution

2. This Constitution is the supreme law of the Republic, law or conduct inconsistent with it is invalid and the obligations imposed by it must be fulfilled

Citizenship

3. (1) There is a common South African citizenship.

   (2) All citizens are -

      (a) equally entitled to the rights, privileges and benefits of citizenship and

      (b) equally subject to the duties and responsibilities of citizenship

   (3) National legislation must provide for the acquisition, loss and restoration of citizenship.

National anthem

4. The national anthem of the Republic is determined by the President by proclamation.

National flag

5. The national flag of the Republic is black, gold, green, white, red and blue, as described and sketed.

Languages

6. (1) The official languages of the Republic are Sepedi. Sesotho, Setswana. SiSwati. Tshivenda. Xitsonga. Afrikaans. English isiNdebele. isiXhosa and isiZulu

(2) Recognising the historically diminished use and status of the indigenous languages of our people, the state must take practical and positive measures to elevate the status and advance the use of these languages.

(3) (a) The national government and provincial governments may use any particular official languages for the purposes of government, taking into account usage, practicality expense regional circumstances and the balance of the needs and preferences of the population as a whole or in the province concerned; but the national government and each provincial government must use at least two official languages.

(b) Municipalities must take into account the language usage and preferences of their residents.

(4) The national government and provincial governments, by legislative and other measures, must regulate and monitor their use of official languages. Without detracting from the provisions of subsection (2). all official languages must enjoy parity of esteem and must be treated equitably.

(5) A Pan South African Language Board established by national legislation must-

(a) promote, and create conditions for the development and use of -

(i) all official languages:

(ii) the Khoi. Nama and San languages: and

(iii) sign language; and

(b) promote and ensure respect for

(i) all languages commonly used by communities in South Africa including German, Greek, Gujarati, Hindi, Portuguese Tamil Telegu and Urdu; and

(ii) Arabic Hebrew Sanskrit and other languages used for religious purposes in South Africa.

Bill of Rights

7. 1. This Bill of Rights is a cornerstone of democracy in south Africa. It enshrines the rights of all people in our country and affirms the democratic values of human dignity, equality and freedom.

2 The state must respect, protect, promote and fulfill the rights in the Bill of Rights Application

8. 1. The Bill of Rights applies to all law, and binds the legislature, the executive, the judiciary and all organs of state.

2. A provision of the Bill of Rights binds a natural or a juristic person if and to the extent that, it is applicable, taking into account the nature of the right and the nature of any duty imposed by the right

3. When applying a provision of the Bill of Rights to a natural or juristic person in terms of a court -

(a) in order to give effect to a right in the Bill must apply or if necessary develop the common law to the extent that legislation does not give effect to that right; and

(b) may develop rules of the common law to limit the right. provided that the limitation is in accordance with section 36(1).

4. A juristic person is entitled to the rights in the Bill of Rights to the extent required by the nature of the rights and the nature of that juristic person

Equality

9. 1. Everyone is equal before the law and has the right to equal protection and benefit of the law

2. Equality includes the full and equal enjoyment of all rights and freedoms To promote the achievement of equality legislative and other measures designed to protect or advance persons, or categories of persons disadvantaged by unfair discrimination may be taken

3. The state may not unfairly discriminate directly or indirectly against anyone on one or mare grounds including race gender sex, pregnancy marital status ethnic or social origin, colour, sexual orientation ace disability religion conscience belief, culture language and birth

4. No person may unfairly discriminate directly or indirectly against anyone on one or more grounds in terms of subsection (3). National legislation must be enacted to prevent or prohibit unfair discrimination

5. Discrimination on one or more of the grounds listed in subsection (3) is unfair unless it is established that the discrimination is fair.

Human dignity

10. Everyone has inherent dignity and the right to have their dignity respected and protected.

Life

11. Everyone has the right to life.

Freedom and security of the person

12. (1) Everyone has the right to freedom and security of the person which includes the right-

(a) not to be deprived of freedom arbitrarily or without just cause.

(b) not to be detained without trial

(c) to be free 38 from all forms of violence from either public or private sources

(d) not to be tortured in any way, and

(e) not to be treated or punished in a cruel, inhuman or degrading way.

(2) Everyone has the right to bodily and psychological integrity which includes the right -

(a) to make decisions concerning reproduction;

(b) to security in and control over their body; and

(c) not to be subjected to medical or scientific experiments without their informed consent

Slavery, servitude and forced labour

13 No one may be subjected to slavery, servitude or forced labour

Privacy

14. Everyone has the right to privacy, which includes the right not to have -

(a) their person or home searched;

(b) their property searched.

(c) their possessions seized; or

(d) the privacy of their communications infringed.

Freedom of religion, belief and opinion

15. (1) Everyone has the right to freedom of conscience, religion, thought, belief and opinion.

(2) Religious observances may be conducted at state or state-aided institutions, provided that -

(a) those observances follow rules made by the appropriate public authorities;

(b) they are conducted on an equitable basis; and

(c) attendance at them is free and Voluntary.

(3) (a) This section does not prevent legislation recognising-

(i) marriages concluded under any tradition, or a system of religious, personal or family law; or

(ii) systems of personal and family law under any tradition, or adhered to by persons professing a particular religion;

(b) Recognition in terms of paragraph (a) must be consistent with this section and the other provisions of the Constitution.

Freedom of expression

16. (1) Everyone has the right to freedom of expression, which includes -

(a) freedom of the press and other media;

(b) freedom to receive or impart information or ideas;

(c) freedom of artistic creativity and

(d) academic freedom and freedom of scientific research.

(2) The right in subsection (1) does not extend to-

(a) propaganda for war

(b) incitement of imminent violence, or

(c) advocacy of hatred that is based on race, ethnicity gender or religion and that constituted incitement to cause harm.

Assembly, demonstration, picket and petition

17 Everyone has the right peacefully and unarmed to assemble, to demonstrate to picket and to present petitions.

Freedom of association

18 Everyone has the right to freedom of association.

Political rights

19 (1) Every citizen is f'ee to make political choices which includes the right-

(a) to form a political party

(b) to participate in the activities of or recruit members for, a political party and

(c) to campaign for a political party or cause.

(2) Every citizen has the right to free fair and regular elections for any legislative body established in terms of the Constitution.

(3) Every adult citizen has the right-

(a) to vote in elections for any legislative body established in terms of the Constitution, and to do so in secret; and

(b) to stand for public office and, if elected to, hold office.

Citizenship

20. No citizen may be deprived of citizenship.

Freedom of movement and residence

21 (1) Everyone has the right to freedom of movement.

(2) Everyone has the right to leave the Republic.

(3) Every citizen has the right to enter to remain in and to reside anywhere in the Republic.

(4) Every citizen has the right to a passport.

Freedom of trade, occupation and profession

22 Every citizen has the right to choose their trade, occupation or profession freely. The practice of a trade, occupation or profession may be regulated by law.

Labour relations

23. (1) Everyone has the right to fair labour practices.

(2) Every worker has the right -

(a) to form and join a trade union;

(b) to participate in the activities and programmes of a trade union; and

(c) to strike.

(3) Every employer has the right -

(a) to form and join an employers' organisation; and

(b) to participate in the activities and programmes of an employers' organisation.

(4) Every trade union and every employers' organisation has the right—

(a) to determine its own administration, programmes and activities;

(b) to organise; and

(c) to form and join a federation.

(5) Every trade union, employers' organisation and employer has the right to engage in collective bargaining. National legislation may be enacted to regulate collective

bargaining. To the extent that the legislation may limit a right in this Chapter, the limitation must comply with section 36(1).

(6) National legislation may recognise union security arrangements contained in collective agreements. To the extent that the legislation may limit a right in this Chapter, the limitation must comply with section 36(1).

Environment

24 Everyone has the right -

(a) to an environment that is not harmful to their health or well-being and

(b) to have the environment protected for the benefit of present and future generations through legislative and other measures that-

(i) prevent pollution and ecological degradation;

(ii) promote conservation; and

(iii) secure ecologically sustainable development and use of natural resources while promoting justifiable economic and social development.

Property

25 (1) No one may be deprived of property except in terms of law of genera! application and no law may permit arbitrary deprivation of property

(2) Property may be expropriated only in terms of law of general application-

(a) for a public purpose or in the public interest; and

(b) subject to compensation the amount of which and the time and manner payment of which have either been agreed to by those or decided or approved by a court

(3) The amount of the compensation and time and manner of payment must be just and equitable reflecting an equitable balance between the public interest and the interests of those affected having regard to all relevant circumstances, including -

(a) the current use of the property;

(b) the history of the acquisition and use of the property:

(c) the market value of the property;

(d) the extent of direct state investment and subsidy in the acquisition and beneficial capital improvement of the property; and

(e) the purpose of the expropriation.

(4) For the purposes of this section -

(a) the public interest includes the nation's commitment to land reform, and to reforms to bring about equitable access to all South Africa's natural resources; and

(b) property is not limited to land.

(5) The state must take reasonable legislative and other measures within its available resources, to foster conditions which enable citizens to gain access to land on an equitable basis.

(6) A person or community whose tenure of land is legally insecure as a result of past racially discriminatory laws or practices is entitled, to the extent provided by an Act of Parliament, either to tenure which is legally secure or to comparable redress.

(7) A person or community dispossessed of property after 19 June 1913 as a result of past racially discriminatory laws or practices is entitled, to the extent provided by an Act of Parliament, either to restitution of that property or to equitable redress.

(8) No provision of this section may impede the state from taking legislative and other measures to achieve land, water and related reform, in order to redress the results of past racial discrimination provided that any departure from the provisions of this section is in accordance with the provisions of section 36(1).

(9) Parliament must enact the legislation referred to in subsection (6).

Housing

26. (1) Everyone has the right to have access to adequate housing.

(2) The state must take reasonable legislative and other measures, within its available resources, to achieve the progressive realisation of this right.

(3) No one may be evicted from their home, or have their home demolished, without an order of court made after considering all the relevant circumstances. No legislation may permit arbitrary evictions.

Health care, food, water and social security

27. (1) Everyone has the right–to have access to

(a) health care services including reproductive health care;

(b) sufficient food and water; and

(c) social security including if they are unable to support themselves and their dependants appropriate social assistance

(2) The state must take reasonable legislative and other measures, within its available resources to achieve the progressive realisation of each of these rights

(3) No one may be refused emergency medical treatment.

Children

28 (1) Every child has the right -

(a) to a name and a nationality from birth;

(b) to family care or parental care, or to appropriate alternative care when removed from the family environment,

(c) to basic nutrition shelter basic health care services and social services

(d) to be Projected from maltreatment neglect, abuse or degradation

(e) to be protected from exploitative labour practices;

(f) not to be required or permitted to perform work or provide services that-

(i) are inappropriate for a person of that child's age; or

(ii) place at risk the child's well-being, education, physical or mental health or spiritual, moral or social development;

(g) not to be detained except as a measure of last resort, in which case in addition to the rights a child enjoys under sections 12 and 35 the child may be detained only for the shortest appropriate period of time, and has the right to be -

(i) kept separately from detained persons over the age of 18 years; and

(ii) treated in a manner, and kept in conditions, that take account of the child's age;

(h) to have a legal practitioner assigned to the child by the state, and at state expense, in civil proceedings affecting the child if substantial injustice would otherwise result; and

(i) not to be used directly in armed conflict, and to be protected in times of armed conflict.

(2) A child's best interests are of paramount importance in every matter concerning the child.

(3) In this section "child" means a person under the age of 18 years.

Education

29. (1) Everyone has the right -

(a) to a basic education, including adult Basic Education, and

(b) to further education, which the state, through reasonable measures, must make progressively available and accessible

(2) Everyone has the right to receive education in the official language or languages of their choice in public educational institutions where that education is reasonably practicable. In order to ensure the effective access to, and implementation of this right, the state must consider all reasonable educational alternatives, including single medium institutions, taking into account -

(a) equity;

(b) practicability; and

(c) the need to redress the results of past racially discriminatory laws and practices.

(3) Everyone has the right to establish and maintain, at their own expense, independent educational institutions that -

(a) do not discriminate on the basis of race;

(b) are registered with the state; and

(c) maintain standards that are not inferior to standards at comparable public educational institutions.

(4) Subsection (3) does not preclude state subsidies for independent educational institutions.

Language and culture

30. Everyone has the right to use the language and to participate in the cultural life of their choice but no one exercising these rights may do so in a manner inconsistent with any provision of the Bill of Rights.

Cultural, religious and linguistic communities

31. (1) Persons belonging to a cultural, religious or linguistic community may not be denied the right with other members of that community –

(a) to enjoy their culture practise their religion and use their language and

(b) to form join and maintain cultural religious and linguistic associations and other organs of civil society

(2) The rights in Subsection (1) may not be exercised in a manner inconsistent with any provision of the Bill of Rights

Access to information

32 (1) Everyone has the right of access to-

(a) any information held by the state and

(b) any information that is held by another person and that is required for the exercise or protection of any rights

(2) National legislation must be enacted to give effect to this right, and may provide for reasonable measures to alleviate the administrative and financial burden on the state

Just administrative action

33. (1) Everyone has the right to administrative action that is lawful, reasonable and procedurally fair.

(2) Everyone whose rights have been adversely affected by administrative action has the right to be given written reasons

(3) National legislation must be enacted to give effect to these rights and must -

(a) provide for the review of administrative action by a court or, where appropriate, an independent and impartial tribunal,

(b) impose a duty on the state to give effect to the rights in subsections (1) and (2); and

(c) promote an efficient administration.

Access to courts

34 Everyone has the right to have any dispute that can be resolved by the application of law decided in a fair public hearing before a court or, where appropriate, another independent and impartial tribunal or forum

Arrested, detained and accused persons

35 (1) Everyone who is arrested for allegedly committing an offence has the right-

(a) to remain silent.

(b) to be informed promptly -

(i) of the right to remain silent; and

(iii) of the consequences of not remaining silent;

(c) not to be compelled to make any confession or admission that could be used in evidence against that person;

(d) to be brought before a court as soon as reasonably possible but not later than -

(i) 48 hours after the arrest; or

(ii) the end of the first court day after the expiry of the 48 hours, if the 48 hours expire outside ordinary court hours or on a day which is not an ordinary court day:

(e) at the first court appearance after being arrested, to be charged or to be informed of the reason for the detention to continue, or to be released, and

(f) to be released from detention if the interests of justice permit subject to reasonable conditions.

(2) Everyone who is detained, including every sentenced prisoner has the right -

(a) to be informed promptly of the reason for being detained,

(b) to choose, and to consult with, a legal practitioner, and to be informed of this right promptly;

(c) to have a legal practitioner assigned to the detained person by the state and at state expense if substantial injustice would otherwise result and to be informed of this right promptly;

(d) to challenge the lawfulness of the detention in person before a court and if the detention is unlawful, to be released;

(e) to conditions of detention that are consistent with human dignity including at least exercise and the provision, at state expense of adequate accommodation, nutrition, reading material and medical treatment; and

(f) to communicate with and be visited by that person's-

(i) spouse or partner

(ii) next of kin

(iii) chosen religious counsellor, and

(iv) chosen medical practitioner

(3) Every accused person has a right to a fair trial which includes the right-

(a) to be informed the charge with sufficient detail to answer it;

(b) to have adequate time and facilities to prepare a defence;

(c) to a public : trial before an ordinary court;

(d) to have their trial begin and conclude without unreasonable delay;

(e) to be present when being tried;

(f) to choose and be represented by a legal practitioner and to be informed of this right promptly;

(g) to have a legal practitioner assigned to the accused person by the state and at state expense if substantial injustice would otherwise result and to be informed of this right promptly;

(h) to be presumed innocent to remain silent, and not to testify during the proceedings;

(i) to adduce and challenge evidence;

(j) not to be compelled to give self-incriminating evidence.

(k) to be tries in a language that the accused person understands or, if that is not practicable, to have the proceedings interpreted in that language;

(l) not to be convicted for an act or omission that was not an offence under either national or international law at the time it was committed or omitted;

(m) not to be tried for an offence in respect of an act or omission for which that person has previously been either acquitted or convicted;

(n) to the benefit of the least severe of the prescribed punishments if the prescribed punishment for the offence has been changed between the time that the offence was committed and the time of sentencing; and

(o) of appeal to, or review by, a higher court.

(4) Whenever this section requires information to be given to a person, that information must be given in a language that the person understands.

(5) Evidence obtained in a manner that violates any right in the Bill of Rights must be excluded if the admission of that evidence would render the trial unfair or otherwise be detrimental to the administration of justice.

Limitation of rights

36 (1) The rights in the Bill of Rights may be limited only in terms of law of general application to the extent that the limitation is reasonable and justifiable in an open and democratic society based on human dignity, equality and freedom, taking into account all relevant factors, including

(a) the nature of the right;

(b) the importance of the purpose of the limitation;

(c) the nature and extent of the limitation;

(d) the relation between the limitation and its purpose; and

(e) less restrictive means to achieve the purpose.

(2) Except as provided in subsection (1) or in any other provision of the Constitution, no law may limit any right entrenched in the Bill of Rights.

States of emergency

37. (1) A state of emergency may be declared only in terms of an Act of Parliament, and only when-

(a) the life of the nation is threatened by war, invasion, general insurrection disorder natural disaster or other public emergency, and

(b) the declaration is necessary to restore peace and order.

(2) A declaration of a state of emergency, and any legislation enacted or other action taken in consequence of that declaration, may be effective only -

(a) prospectively; and

(b) for no more than 21 days from the date of the declaration, unless the National Assembly resolves to extend the declaration The Assembly may extend a declaration of a state of emergency for no more than three months at a time. The first extension of the state of emergency must be by a resolution adopted with a supporting vote of a majority of the members of the Assembly. Any subsequent extension must be by a resolution adopted with a supporting vote of at least 60 per cent of the members of the Assembly. A resolution in terms of this paragraph may be adopted only following a public debate in the Assembly.

(3) Any competent court may decide on the validity of -

(a) a declaration of a state of emergency;

(b) any extension of a declaration of a state of emergency; or

(c) any legislation enacted, or other action taken, in consequence of a declaration of a state of emergency.

(4) Any legislation enacted in consequence of a declaration of a state of emergency may derogate from the Bill of Rights only to the extent that -

(a) the derogation is strictly required by the emergency; and

(b) the legislation -

(i) is consistent with the Republic's obligations under international law applicable to states of emergency:

(ii) conforms to subsection (5); and

(iii) is published in the national Government Gazette as soon as reasonably possible after being enacted

(5) No Act of Parliament that authorises a declaration of a state of emergency and no legislation enacted or other action taken in consequence of a declaration may permit or authorise-

(a) indemnifying the state, or any person, in respect of any unlawful act;

(b) any derogation from this section; or

(c) any derogation from a section mentioned in column 1 of the Table of Non-Derogable Rights, to the extent indicated opposite that section in column 3 of the Table

(6) Whenever anyone is detained without trial in consequence of a derogation of rights resulting from a

declaration of a state of emergency, the following conditions must be observed:

(a) An adult family member or friend of the detainee must be contacted as soon as reasonably possible, and informed that the person has been detained.

(b) A notice must be published in the national Government Gazette within five days of the person being detained stating the detainees name and place of detention and referring to the emergency measure in terms of which that person has been detained.

(c) The detainee must be allowed to choose, and be visited at any reasonable time by a medical practitioner.

(d) The detainee must be allowed to choose, and be visited at any reasonable time by, a legal representative.

(e) A court must review the detention as soon as reasonably possible, but no later than 10 days after the date the person was detained, and the court must release the detainee unless it is necessary to continue the detention to restore peace and order.

(f) A detainee who is not released in terms of a review under paragraph (e), or who is not released in terms of a review under this paragraph, may apply to a court for a further review of the detention at any time after 10 days have passed since the previous review, and the court must release the detainee unless it is still necessary to continue the detention to restore peace and order.

(g) The detainee must be allowed to appear in person before any court considering the detention, to be represented by a legal practitioner at those hearings, and to make representations against continued detention.

Table of Non-Derogable Rights

Section number	*Section Title*	*Extent to which the right is protected*
9	Equality	With respect to unfair discrimination solely on the grounds of race, colour ethnic or social origin sex religion or language
10	Human dignity	Entirely
11	Life	Entirely
12	Freedom and security of the person	With respect to subsection (1) (d) and (e) and (2) (c)
13	Slavery servitude and forced labour	With respect to slavery and servitude
28	Children	With respect to Subsection (1) (d) and (e) the rights in subparagraphs (i) and (ii) of Subsection (1) (g) and Subsection 1 (ii) in respect of Children of 15 years and younger
35	Arrested detained and accused persona	With respect tp Subsection (1) (a) (b) and (c) and (2) (d) the rights in paragraphs (a) (0) of subsection (3) excluding paragraph (d) subsection (4) and subsection (5) with respect to the exclusion of evidence if the admission of that evidence would render the trial unfair

(h) The state must present written reasons to the court to justify the continued detention of the detainee, and must give a copy of those reasons to the detainee at least two days before the court reviews the detention.

(7) If a court releases a detainee that person may not be detained again on the same grounds unless the state first shows a court good cause for re-detaining that person.

(8) Subsections (6) and (7) do not apply to persons who are not South African citizens and who are detained in consequence of an international armed conflict instead the state must comply with the standards binding on the Republic under international humanitarian law in respect of the detention of such persons.

Enforcement of rights

38. Anyone listed in this section has the right to approach a competent court alleging that a right in the Bill of Rights has been infringed or threatened and the court may grant appropriate relief including a declaration of rights. The persons who may approach a court are-

(a) anyone acting in their own interest

(b) anyone acting on behalf of another person who cannot act in their own name.

(c) anyone acting as a member of or in the interest of a group or class of persons.

(d) anyone acting in the public interest and

(e) an association acting in the interest of its members.

Interpretation of Bill of Rights

39. (1) When interpreting the Bill of Rights a court tribunal or forum-

(a) must promote the values that underlie an open and democratic society based on human dignity equality and freedom

(b) must consider international law, and

(c) may consider foreign law

(2) When interpreting any legislation and when developing the common law or customary law every court tribunal or forum must promote the spirit purport and objects of the Bill of Rights.

(3) The Bill of Rights does not deny the existence of any other rights or freedoms that are recognised or conferred by common law, customary law or legislation, to the extent that they are consistent with the Bill.

8

Conclusion

The contemporary periou witnesses the democratic form of government as one of the best system of governance. The democratic norms, and the institutions (executive, legislative and judiciary) related to it recognises throughout the world. The post 1990 phase highlights the democratic pattern througout the world, mainly in the Eastern Europe, Asia and Africa. Most of the African countries during the last decade turned towards the democratic government from the military or autocratic rule. The Southern African countries like Angola, Botswana, Mozambique, Namibia, Zimbabwe and South Africa has adopted one or other form of democratic governments in this phase. South Africa, one of the important region here, had came forward strongly in favour of democratic process in the post 1990 period. After the lengthy negotiations and discussions regarding the form of democracy within the country, agreed to adopt a Constitution in 1994. The Constitution clearly reflects the idea of centralized government with the provision to share some important powers with the provincial and at local level. One may say that the Constitution of South Africa depicts the features of centralized federation.

Federalism being a popular form of democratic system is well researched and well studied subject around the globe. Various scholars have defined and elaborated the concept of federalism in different ways, adopting different methods and analyzed it differently. There is a consensus around the world on federalism which shows the distribution or shares of power either at two levels (centre and local) or at three levels (Centre, State or Province and local). Alongwith it, both the form of governments either unitary or federal, has practised the ways of sharing of power like in England, US, Switzerland, Canada and so on. It is important to note here that one can analyze the process of federalism by analyzing its pattern or form of government.

Federalism has taken its entry in South Africa only after 1994. Though South Africa had got independence from her imperial masters in 1910, but it took a very long period of about eighty four years to make South Africa governed by majority people. The society needs a democratic transformation to achieve basic facilities which is still under the process. The white people, which were in minority reigned South Africa during the past eight decades. The party system represented by the white people and the black people (majority) was neglected and ignored by these parties. National party was the mostimportant party which remained in power for considerably a longer period of time. During this period several anti-black acts were passed and indigenous African people were deprived their policies to remain in power and keep the black people away from it. Though in 1912 South African Native National Congress (SAANC), come into existence as a movement against the atrocities of the white regime. But this movement could only scratch the surface of the possibility to check the government to carry on its exploitative policies. ANC was banned in 1960 by the government when it became a challenge to the white power. But it continued to carry its resistant movement. During this period South Africans endured the exploitation which came forward in different forms, like the land act of 1913, the Native Acts of 1923, the Population Registration Act of 1950, the Group Areas Act of 1950, the Bantustan Schemes and the Prohibition of Mixed Marriage Act 1949 and the Separate Amenities Act of 1950 by which the rights of majority people, were snatched. The 1976 Soweto massacre showed the ugliest face of the oppressive government. But the ANC carried on its movement for the restoration of the rights of blacks people. But it was not succeeded until 1994 that a democratic South Africa came into existence by the efforts of the ANC and the positive initiatives taken by the President de Clerk of the National Party. The democratic South Africa adopted the federal form of government in 1994.

Though, there had been a long tradition of federalism for whites minority in South Africa, but the 1910 onwards it emerged as a counter ideology to apartheid, which was being advocated by ruling parties. Hence, the concept and practice of the federalism in South Africa has had a number of different and untraditional connotations. Various parties have analysed the federalism, keeping in view their respective ideologies. There are a number of political parties today which occupy a crucial place in the political scene of South Africa. African National Congress (ANC), no doubt is the most significant party out of them. Alongwith it, the Inkatha Freedom Party (IFP), New National Party (NNP), Democratic Party and South African Communist Party (SACP) also hold significant positions in the political scene of South Africa. Pan-Africanist Congress (PAC), Azanian People's Organization (AZAPO), Freedom Front (FF), United Democratic Movement (UDM) and African Christian Democratic Party (ACDP) are also worthy of mention. These parties are having a different view and the ideologies related to it on the nature of state in South Africa. The ANC which is in power supports unitary system and does not very much in favour of federalism. Though the governments claims to be a unitary state but it reflects the features of a federal state. The constitution clearly demonstrates the division of power in each sphere of governance which again strengthen the idea of federal state. The National Party (NP) which came in power in 1948 and strengthen the policy of apartheid through oppressive methods, is now committed to a non-racial, non-sexist, multiparty democracy that recognizes the central role of the family and the community. The principle such as law and order, rule of law, a free enterprise economy with social responsibility, inclusive government and federalism are the foundations of party's platform. The party proposes a three tier government in which full legislative, executive and judicial functions are conferred on central, provincial and regional local authority.

The Inkatha Freedom Party which claims to have grown from cultural organization in 1920, regards itself as upholding democratic principles and does not want a centralised state. But the party acknowledges the constitution as the "supreme law of the state' and firmly believes in the concept of judicial review and true guarantee of political rights of all groups. The administration of law and justice should be carried out in a fair and impartial way in the interest of the individual. The Democratic Party which came into existence in 1989 after the merger of former progressive Federal Party, Independent Party and National Democratic Movement could win only 10 seats in the 1994 general elections. Democratic Party now fights for the protection of human rights and the extension of federalism and free enterprise in South Africa. It supports a central government having limited authority and power. It strengthens the authorities in various spheres of governance in order to bring the people closer to it. It favours more and maximum powers to the different provinces specially economic power along with the political one. It refers to an independent judiciary and the rule of law.

The Azanian People's Organization (AZAPO) believes that AZANIA (South Africa) is a unitary state. It rejects the balkanization of AZANIA to separate semi-autonomous units. The AZAPO government will seek to abolish provincial government as presently constituted and consolidate the country into few provinces with administrative functions of governments carrying out central government policies and directions. The SACP is one of the main partners of ANC in central government, but as a SACP, it does not participate in electoral politics. The SACP favours a unitary state having limited united powers to the provinces. It recognizes

Reconstruction and Development Programme (RDP) as instrument of social transformation. Over all, the idea of federalism is not the choice of SACP. Unlike the other parties of South Africa the Pan-African Congress (PAC) desires to unite all Black Africans in a single national front.

The CODESA has been a milestone in the way to establish democracy in South Africa. It has worked towards the creation of climate for free political participation. It is evident that various parties have their own ideology to restore democracy and federalism in South Africa. Though, the Constitution provides substantial powers to the provinces, but the ruling party favours a highly centralized federal state. This particular fact is bound to influence the nature of federalism in South Africa.

Democracy is not just all about political change. It does have social dimension as well. The civil society has been influenced by the democratic changes and vice-versa in South Africa. It express a scepticism towards a statist policies which has dominated in independent South Africa. Civil society in the South Africa is emerging institutions with strong democratic commitments. There are tensions inherent in both the liberal and radical definitions of civil society between citizens autonomy and state coercion. The imperative of autonomy presumably requires that as few liberties as possible be circumscribed. As for the ethnicity is concerned it has served as a factor of division in South Africa social system. The policy of apartheid precluded the establishment of true democracy in South Africa. Though this apartheid policy has been official scraped, there is a need to strengthen civil society. This phase witnessed violence among different tribal groups, demand of an independent African state, status of traditional leaders, language rights and demands for independent Kwazulu state. As far as the party politics is concerned ANC, PAC and SACP negotiated with the interest groups of the ethnic leaders. The South African Constitution particularly the Bill of Rights has provided such an opportunity so that the interest of each group could be taken care of. It also promotes and creates conditions for the development and use of different languages that exist in South Africa.

Religion has also a crucial and central role to play in the politics of South Africa. Though the Constitution provides for the equality of religions, but the section on the freedom of religions and in the rights of cultural, linguistic and religions communities are controversial in the sense of their extent and content.

Alongwith the ethnic problems, there is a constant threat of other related issues like land redistribution, housing problem, employment, education and health facilities are other need an immediate attention to strengthen civil society. Redistribution is another crucial aspects of the problem which is being dealt with tremendous care. The ANC supports the right to own property but stresses the need for the redistribution of land through state owned land. The Reconstruction and Development Programme (RDP) calls for 30 per cent of South Africa's land to be redistribution over the next five years. Alongwith it, the ANC has promised to build at least 1 million low cost houses in five years. The party also vowed to transform and upgrade the 411 migrant workers' hostels which will house 1 million residents and will bring electricity to at least 2.5 million houses by the end of 2000. The government is also concerned with the economic recession and rising unemployment. A recent white paper of the government proposes provision of a maximum grant of R. 12,800 for those earning less than R. 1,500 a month. Most gage identity insurance scheme, with the capital provided by government and foreign aid and the scheme maintained by users premiums. Bank will be issued against non-payments of loans or if they are unable to repossess loans because of violence of political conditions. It also proposed consumer protection measures to prevent speculation and ensuring quality control. The Truth and Reconciliation Commission (TRC) is another step formed in this direction. From the August 1995, the TRC heard representation from political parties. The TRC is an attempt to ensure the justice to the victims of apartheid.

It reluctantly offers qualified apologies that served only to embarrass, themselves and anger their victims. The NP had perfected apartheid and used religion to justify it. On the other hand, ANC fought apartheid tooth and nail on the grounds of universal morality. The NP and ANC hold different and opposite views in this issues. The Inkatha Freedom Party (IFP) supports the social issues, which was raised by ANC in the RDP documents. It also supports better education, health, employment, housing and other issues.

Civic society needs a democratic form of government and it is true in a country like South Africa, where the saplings of democracy need to be strengthened. The multiparty system provides an adhesive force to the democracy. It is true that any good democracy needs a strong opposition as well as a ruling party within the multiparty framework, but South Africa currently does not carry a strong opposition party. The opposition parties mainly the Democratic Party and the New National Party are trying to provide a strong opposition through their alliance. This Democratic Alliance is pursuing hard to make alliance with the other parties but mainly with the IFP. The positive opposition through scientific and logical criticism really strengthen the democratic pattern in South Africa.

Over all, all the political parties are in favour to solve the social problems. The existing imbalance in society should be the priority of ruling party and opposition parties can contribute its positive role. The opposition parties put a check on the proper distribution of social needs which will help in the distribution to the real needy persons. They can cross check the use or misuse of financial allocation to social sector. The land redistribution should be placed a top priority in the government's agenda. The process has already been started but it need to be speed it up. The process needs a care in the redistribution otherwise South Africa can face the Zimbabwean crisis on its land. Along with the land, the other issues also need utmost care. The economic policies like GEAR should concentrate on the growth on the one hand and redistribution on the other. The government claims that the GEAR has taken over the objective of the RDP. How much it will be relevant is the matter of time.

To sum up, the democratic forces in South Africa inevitably sidelined the forces which leads to social disruption, conflict and violence. After the nine decades of authoritarian rule, the democratic forces bolsters the moral forces of representative government. The hopes of the whole world particularly the African continent will help South Africa to move in the direction which lead to political stability and strengthen democracy.

Bibliography

Books

Adam, Heribert, *Modernizing Racial Domination* (Los Angeles, California University Press, 1971).

– and Hermann Ciliomee, *Ethnic, Power Mobilised : Can South Africa Change ?* (New Haven, Yale University Press, 1979).

– and Kogilo Moodley, *South Africa without apartheid : Dismantling Racial Domination* (Berkeley, University of California Press, 1986).

Almond, G.A. & Coleman, J.S. Ceds), *The Politics of Developing Areas* (Princeton, Princeton University Press, 1960).

– G. & Verba, *The Civic Culture* (Princeton, Princeton University Press, 1963).

Amin, S., *Delinking* (New York, Monthly Review Press, 1985).

Aptor, O., *The Potetics of Citizenship and Immigration in the New Europe* (Middlesex, University Migrants Project, 1997).

Balibar, E. & Wallersteni, *Race, Nation and Class* (Ambiguous Identities, Verso Books, London, 1991).

Baskim, J., *Against the Current : Labour and Economic Policy in South Africa* (Johnnesburg, Ravan Press, 1996).

Beaudet, P. & Theade, *Southern Africa after Apartheid ?* (MacMillan, London, 1994).

Beckman, B. & Marais, *Popular Movement and the Struggler for Transformation in South Africa* (Alternatives, Montreal, 1994).

Blackburn, R., *After the Fall : The Failure of Communism and the Future of Socialism* (Yerso Books, London, 1991).

Bond, P., *Commanding Heights and Community Control : New Economics for a New South Africa* (Johnnesburg, Pavan Press, 1991).

Cohen, J. & Arato, *Civil Society and Political Theory* (Cambridge, Massachwetts, MIIT Press, 1960).

Cole, J., *Cross Roads : The Politics of Reform and Repression 1976-1986* (Johnnesburg, Ravan Press, 1987).

Davies, R., *Integration or Cooperation in a Post-Apartheid South Africa* (Centre for Southern African Studies, Cape Town, 1992).

Dahl, R., *Democracy and Its Critics* (New Nahen, Yale University Press, 1989).

Diamond, L., Linz J. & Lipset, S.M., *Democracy in Developing Countries* (Boulder, Colorado, Lynne Rienner, 1994).

Dyvenage, M., *The Idea of Politics* (London, Methuen, 1967).

Ellis, S. & Sechaba, T., *Comrades against Apartheid : The ANC and the South African Communist Party in Exile* (James Currey & Indiana University Press, London, Bloomington, 1992).

Epstein, L.D., *Political Parties in Western Democracies* (New York Praeger, 1967).

Faure, M. & Lane, J.E., *South Africa : Designing New Political Institution* (London, Sage, 1996).

Friedman, S. (ed.), *The Long Journey : South Africa's Quest for a Negotiated Settlement* (Ravan Press, Johnnesburg, 1987).

Gann, L.H. and Peter Duignan, *Why South Africa will Survive* (London, Croom Helm, 1981).

Geldenhuys, Deon, *The Diplomacy of Isolation* (Johnnesburg, MacMillan, 1984).

Geurtiz, C, *The Integrative Revolution : Primordial Sentiments and Civic Justice* (California, Wadworth Publishing, 1967).

Hamilton, G. & Mare, G., *The Inkatha Freedom Party : In Election 94 South Africa* (London, James Currey, 1994).

Held, D., *Models of Democracy* (Cambridge, Polity Press, 1996). Heather Deegan, *South Africa Reborn* (London, UCL Press, 1999).

Horowitz, D., *A Democratic South Africa* (Berkeley University of California Press, 1991).

Johnston, R.W. & Schlemmer, *Launching Democracy in South Africa* (New Hanen, Yale University Press, 1996).

Kahan, B., *Exchange Control Liberalisation in South Africa* (Cape Town TD ASA, 1996).

Kariel H. (ed.) *Frontiers of Democratic Theory* (New York, Syracuse University Press, 1970).

Keane, J., *Civil Society and the State* (Verso Books, London, 1988). Keane, J., *Democracy and Civil Society* (Verso Books, London, 1988).

Laslau, E. & Mouffe, *Hegemony and Socialist Strategy : Towards a Radical Democratic Politics* (London, Verso Books, 1985).

Lijphort, A., *Democracy in Plural Societies : A Comparatives Exploration* (New Haner : Yale University Press, 1977).

Lipton, M., Ellis, F. & Lipton, *Land, Labour and Livelihoods in Rural South Africa* (Durban, Indicator Press, 1996).

Lodge, T., *South Africa : Democracy and Development in a Post-apartheid Society* (Cambridge, Polity Press, 1996).

Lodge, T. & Nasson, B., *South Africa : Time Running Out* (United States, Ford Foundation, 1991).

Maris, D., *South Africa : Constitutional Development; A Multidisciplinary Approach* (Johnnesburg, Southern, 1989).

Maylam, Paul, *A History of the African People of South Africa* (London, Crrom Helm, 1989).

Meli, Francis, *A History of the ANC South Africa belong to Us* (Harare, Zimbabwean Publishing House, 1988).

Mbeki, G. *The Struggle for Liberation in South Africa : A Short History* (Dakid Philip, Cape Town, 1992).

Minaar, A. de v., *Conflict and Violence in Natal/Kwa Zulu : Historical Perspectives* (Pretoria, Human Sciences Research Council, 1990).

Nattrass, J., *The South African Economy : Its Growth and Change* (Oxford University Press, Cape Town, 1988).

Nattrass, N. & Frdington, *The Political Economy of South Africa* (Oxford University Press, Cape Town, 1990).

Nafziger, E.W., *The Debt Crisis in Africa* (The Johns HopKins University Press, Baltimore and London, 1993).

Neumann, S., *European and Comparative Government* (New York, McGraw Hill Press, 1960).

Nolutshugu, Sam, *Changing South Africa* (Manchester, Manchester University Press, 1982).

O, Meara, D., *The Apartheid State and the Politics of the National Party* (Johnnesburg, Ravan Press, 1996).

O, Meara, D., *Volkskapitalism : Class, Capital and Ideology in the Development of Afrikaner Nationalism 1934-1948* (Johnnesburg, Ravan Press, 1983).

O, Donnell, G. & Schmitter, P.C., *Transition from Authoriain Rule : Tentative Conclusions about uncertain Democracies* (Baltimore, John's Hopkins University Press, 1986).

Ottaway, M., *The Struggle for a New Order* (Washington D.C. the Brooking Institute, 1993).

Price, R.M., *The Apartheid State in Crisis : Political Transformation in South Africa : 1975 : 1990* (New York, Oxford University Press, 1991).

Sparks, A., *Tomorrow is Another Country : The Inside Story of South Africa's Negotiated Revolution* (Sandton, B. Struik Book Distributors, 1994).

Saxena, S.C., *Foreign Policy of African States : Politics of Dependence and Confrontation* (Delhi, Deep and Deep Publications, 1982).

Shrivastava, A.K., *Churche and Apartheid* (Delhi, P.B.D. Publications, 1989).

Smith, Jack Shaphered, *Buthelezi* (Melville, Hans Strydom Publications, 1989).

Stadler, A., *The Political Economy of Modern South Africa* (Cape Town, David Philip, 1987).

Suttner, R. & Cronin J., *Thirty Years of the Freedom Charter* (Ravan Press, Johannesburg, 1986).

Turok, B. *Development in South Africa : In South Africa : Within or Apart* (London, Zed Press, 1997).

Unterhalter, E., *Class, Race and Gender in South Africa in Guertian* (Cambridge, University of Cambridge Press, 1989).

Forced Removal : The Division, Segregation and Control of the *People of South Africa* (London, International Reference and Aid Fund for Southern Africa, 1987).

Yuurren, D.J., *South Africa in the Nineties* (Pretoria, HSRC Publishers, 1991).

Webster, E., *Democratic Consolidation in Southern Africa* (Witwater and University of Witwatrand Press, 1996).

Weiner, M., *Political Integration and Political Development in Political Modernisation* (California, Wadsworth Publishing Co., 1967).

Welch, C., *Political Modernisation* (California, Wadsworth Publishing Co., 1967).

Welsh, D., *The South African Elections* (London, RIIA Press, 1994).

White, C, *Democratic Societies and Voluntary Associations and Democratic Culture in a South African Township* (Johnnesburg, Centre for Policy Studies, 1995).

Wiseman, J.A., *Democracy in Black Africa : Survival and Revival* (New York, Paragon House, 1990).

Williams, D. & Young, T. *Civil Society and Democratisation* (Warwick, British International Studies Association, 1993).

Worden, N., *The Making of Modern South Africa* (Oxford, Blackwell, 1995).

Articles

Anon, "Prospects for a Negotiated Settlement", *African Communist* (Johannesburg), No. 122, 3rd Quarter, 1990.

Barrel, N., "The Turn to the Masses : The African National Congress's Strategic Review of 1978-79", *Journal of Southern African Studies* (New York), Vol. 18, No. 1, March, 1991.

Baylies, C., "Political Conditionality and Democratisation", *Review of African Political Economy* (Pretoria), Vol. 22, No. 65, 1995.

Bhaunik, Prashun, "Nelson Mandela : Marriah to Missanary", *The Times of India* (Delhi) 18 March 1990.

Boadshow, Y.W. and Tshandu, Z., "Foreign Capital Penetration State Intervention and Development in Sub-Saharan Africa", *International Studies Quarterly*, Vol. 34, No. 2, 1990.

Carrin Yunus, "Trade Unionism in Natal : Shop Floor Relations between Indian and African Workers", *South African Labour Bulletin,* Vol. 11(4) : Feb-March 1986.

Chandan, Ramesh, "Problem Mount for Nelson Mandela", *The Sunday Times of India,* 14 October, 1990.

Clocte, Fanci, "Policy Impact of Democracy in South Africa", African Insight (butoria), Vol. 21 (4): 1991.

– 'Negotiating Political Change" in Neimmeifer and F. Clocte, eds.

Dynamics of Negotiations in South Africa (Pretoria, HSRC Publishers, (1991).

Davies, R., "Integration or Co-operation in a Post-Apartheid South Africa", *Centre for Southern African Studies* (Cape Town), 1992.

Dhlomo, Oscar, "Factors Influencing Change in South Africa," Clarion Call (Durban), Vol. 3 : 1990.

Gupta, Aniruda, "Sanctions against South Africa", India Quarterly (Delhi), Vol. , No. 11 (3), July-Sept., 1986.

Legum, Colin, "South Africa : The Way Forward", *New Africa* (London), No. 283: April 1991.

Lemrdual, R., African Transitions to Democracy : An Interim Assessment", *Africa Insight* (Pretoria), Vol. 22, No. 3, 1992.

Mboweni, T., "Formulating Policy for a Democratic South Africa : Some Observation", *Institute for Development Studies Bulletin* (Sussex), Vol. 25, No. 1, 1994.

Morns, M., "State Capital and Growth : The Political Economy of the National Question" in S. Culb (ed.) *South Africa's Economic Crisis* (Cape Town, David Philip, 1991).

Ottoway, M., "Liberation Movements and Democracy", *Journal of Modern African Studies* (Cambridge), Vol. No. 3, 1991.

Sawant, Ankush, B., "The Organization of African Unity and Liberation Struggle", *Africa Quarterly* (Delhi), Vol. 25, No. 3&4.

Sidler, Peter, "South Africa : The Rocky Road to Reform", *Swiss Review of International Affairs* (Zurich), Vol. 33(1), March, 1984.

Singh, Harjinder, "Winds of Change in south Africa", *The Hindustan Times* (New Delhi), Vol. 37 (12) : December 1981.

___, "Reform in South Africa a Tangled Web:, *Contemporary Review* (London), Vol. 244(1416) : January 1984.

Toussant, "On Workersian, Socialism and Communist Party", *African Communist* (Johannesburg), No. 114, 3rd October, 1988.

Tutu, Derund, "Ref. Erendum was a Kacist Shop", *The Hindustan Times* (New Delhi), 22 March, 1992.

Yenkatsubhiah, H., "India and Apartheid Question", *India Quarterly* (Delhi), Vol. 33(1): Jan-March, 1977.

Walalmeni, Patti, "South Africa : The Unthinkable Starts to Look Inucitable", *The Times of India* (Delhi), 6th January, 1990.

Weinnar, H., "Political Litigation and Political Development" in C. Welch ed., *Political Modernization* (California, Wadsworth Publishing Co., 1967).

Welch, D., "The Democratic Party", in Reynolds, A., ed. *Election '94 South Africa: The Campaigns, Results and Future Prospects* (Cape Town, David Philip, 1994).

Welch, D., "Towards an Analysis of the South African State", *International Journal of Sociology of the Law* (London), No. 8, 1980.

Wolpe, H., "Strategic Issues in the Struggle for National Liberation in South Africa" *Socialist Review* (Pretoria), Vol. 8, No. 2, 1984.

Zita, I., "Unity of the Left", *African Communist* (Johnnesburg), No. 132 (2nd Quarter), 1993.

"Moving Beyond the Social Contract", *Africm Communist* (Johnnesburg), 134 (3rd Quarter), 1993.

Primary Source

Budget Review 1998, 1999, Department of Finance Government of South Africa 2000.

Convention for a Democratic South Africa (CODESA) WGZ, Government of South Africa, 1994.

Government of South Africa, Umamyans Publications, Johannesburg 1994.

Growth Employment and Redistribution, Ministry Finance, Government of South Africa, 1999.

Inter Governmental Relation (The Department of Constitutional and Provincial Affairs, Pretoria, May 1999.

Reconstruction Development Programme, White Paper. South of Sahara, Europa Publication, 1999.

The Constitution of South Africa.

Books

Adam, *Heribert, Modernizing Racial Domination* (Los Angeles, California University Press, 1971).

—and Hermann *Ciliomee, Ethnic, power Mobilised: Can South Africa change*? (New Haven, Yale University Press, 1979).

—and Kogila Moodley, *South Africa without Apartheid: Dismantling Racial Domination* (Berkeley, University of California Press, 1986).

Asoyan, Boris, *Apartheid- the White Man's Burden* (Moscow, Progress Publishers, 1988).

Benjamin, Anne, Winnie Mandela (London, Penguin Books, 1984).

Benson, Mary, *South Africa: The Straggle for a Birthright* (London, International Defence and Aid Fund for Southern Africa, 1985).

Berger, Peter and Bobby Godsell, *A Future South Africa* (Cape Town, Human and Rousseau, 1980).

Bernstein, Hilda, *For Their Triumphs and for Their Tears* (London, International Defence and Aid Fund for Southern Africa, 1985).

Butheiezi, Mangosuthu G., *South Africa: My Vision of the Future* (London, Weidenfeld and Nicolson. 1990).

David. S., *Apartheid Rebels: Inside South Africa's hidden war* (New Haven, Yale, University Press, 1987).

Gann, L.H. and Peter Duignan, *Why South Africa will survive* (London, Groom Helm, 1981).

Geldenhuys, Deon, *The Diplomacy of Isolation* (Johannesburg, Macmillan, 1984).

Giliomee, H. and L. Schlemmer, *From apartheid to nation-building* (Cape Town, Oxford University Press, 1990).

—,eds., *Negotiating South Africa's Future* (Johannesburg, Southern Book Publishers, 1989).

Hanlon, Joseph and Roger Omond, *The Sanctions Handbook* (London, Penguin Books, 1987).

Haysom, Nicholas, *Apartheid's Private Army: The Rise of Right-wing Vigilantes in South Africa* (London, Catholic Institute of International Relations, 1986).

Ikle, F.C., *How Nations Negotiate* (London, Harper and Row, 1964).

Kock, Wessel De, *Usuthu ! Cry Peace*! (Cape Town, Open Hand Press, 1986).

Legum, Colin, *The Battiefronts of Southern Africa* (New York, London, Africana Publishing Co., 1988).

Lijphart, A., *Democracy in Plural Societies* (New Haven, Yale University Press, 1977).

—,*Power-sharing in South Africa* (Berkley, Institute of International Studies, 1988).

Lodge, Tom, *Black politics in South Africa since 1945* (Johannesburg, Ravan Press, 1983).

Mandela, Nelson, *The Struggle is my life* (London, International Defence and Aid Fund for Southern Africa, 1978).

—,*No Easy Walk to Freedom* (Oxford, Heinemann, 1989).

Marais, D., *South Africa; Constitutional Development; A multi-disciplinary approach* (Johannesburg, Southern, 1989).

Maylam, Paul, *A History of the African People of South Africa* (London, Croom Helm, 1986).

Mee r, Fatima, ed., *Resistance in the Townships* (Durban, Madiba Publications, 1989).

— ,ed., *Treason Trial - 1985* (Durban, Madiba Publications, 1989).

Meli, Francis, *A History of the ANC: South Africa belong to us* (Harare, Zimbabwean Publishing House, 1988).

Minaar, A. de V., *Conflict and Violence in NatalIKwaZulu: Historical Perspectives* (Pretoria, Human Sciences Research Council, 1990).

Mzala, *Gatsha Buthelezi: Chief with a double agenda* (London/ New Jersey, Zed Books Ltd., 1986).

Nolutshugu, Sam, *Changing South Africa* (Manchester, Manchester University Press, 1982).

Ramamurthi, T.G., *Fight against apartheid* (Delhi, ABC Publishing House, 1984).

Reddy, E.S., *Apartheid: The United Nations and the International Community* (Delhi, Vikas Publishing House, 1986).

Rogers, Barbara, *D.I.V.I.D.E. and Rule* (London, International / Defence and Aid Fund, 1980).

Saxena, S.C., *Foreign Policy of African States: Politics of dependence and confrontation* (Delhi, Deep and Deep Publications, 1982).

—,*Political Conflicts and Power in Africa* (Delhi, UDH Publishers, 1985).

Shrivastava, A.K., *Churches and Apartheid* (Delhi, P.B.D. Publications, 1989).

Smith, Jack Shephered, *Buthelezi* (Melville, Hans Strydom Publications, 1989).

Stadler, A. *The Political economy of modern South Africa* (Cape I Town, David Philip, 1987).

Unterhalter, Elaine, *Forced Removal: The Division, Segregation and Control of the People of South Africa* (London, Internationa! Defence and Aid Fund for Southern Africa, 1987).

Vuurren D.J. van, et at, eds., *South Africa in the Nineties* (Pretoria, HSRC Publishers, 1991).

Wiseman, J.A., *Democracy in black Africa: Survival and revival* (New York, Paragon 1990).

Articles

"Africa: Winds of Change", *Africa Confidential* (London), Vol. 31 (5): 9 March 1990,p.1.

Aitchison, J.J.W., "The Civil war in Natal" in G. Moss and I. Obery, eds., *South African Review* (Johannesburg, Ravan, 1989).

Anglin, Douglas G., "Southern African responses to Eastern European developments", *Journal of Modern African Studies* (Cambridge), Vol. 28(3) : 1990.

Bhaumik,Prashun, "Nelson Mandela : Messiah to Missionary", *The Times of India* (Delhi), 18 March 1990.

Carrim, Yunus, "Trade Unionism in Natal: Shopfloor relations between Indian and African workers", *South African Labour Bulletin* , Vol. 11 (4): Feb.-March 1986, pp. 44-64.

–,"The Constitutional trap", *Post Natal* (Durban), 3-6 June 1987.

Chandran, Ramesh, "Problems mount for Nelson Mandela", *The Sunday Times of India*, 14 October 1990.

Cloete, Fanie, "Policy impact of democracy in South Africa", *Africa Insight* (Pretoria), Vol. 21 (4): 1991, pp. 222-32.

"Characteristics of political change in South Africa: 1980-1990" in F. Cloete, L. Schlemmer and D van Vuuren, eds., *Policy option for a new South Africa,* (Pretoria, HSRC Publishers 1991).

– ,"Negotiating political change" in L. Nievumeijer and F. Cloete, eds., *Dynamics of negotiation in South Africa* (Pretoria, HSRC Publishers, 1991).

Davies, Robert, " South African State Strategy in the period since 2 February 1990", a paper presented to an international seminar on " South Africa and the World", organized by African Studies Society of India, New Delhi, on 19-21 February 1991. (Unpublished)

De Klerk Frederik W., "Sanctions retard social progress", *The Hindustan Times* (Delhi), 9 July 1990.

Dhlomo, Oscar, "Factors influencing change in South Africa", *Clarion Call* (Durban), Vol. 3: 1990, pp. 12-14,16.

–"Inkakha's standpoint on negotiations", Clarion Call, Vol. 3: 1990, pp.17-19.

– ,"The Government and the ANC", *Natal Witness* (Pietermaritzburg), 11 April 1991.

– ,"The ANC-PAC Patriotic Front," *Natal Witness*, 1 May 1991.

– ,"Pre-requisites for peace", *Natal Witness*, 30 May 1991.

– ,"Tactical Twists", *Sunday Tribune* (Durban), 30 June 1991.

Gopal, Ajit S., "Why Pretoria caved in", *The Hindustan Times*, 2 February 1990.

Gupta, Anirudha, "Sanctions against South Africa", *India Quarterly* (Delhi), Vol. XLII (3): July-Sept, 1986, pp. 274-83.

Gwala, N., "Class alternatives in the struggle against Inkatha", *South African Labour Bulletin*, Vol. 13 (3): March/April 1988.

Hogg, Andrew and Richard Ellis, " De Klerk walks the tight-rope of shared power", *The.Times of India* , 9 February , 1990.

Johnson, Shaun, "ANC's halo is slipping", *The Star* (Johannesburg), 19 July 1991.

Laurence, Patrick, "Another coup by De Klerk", *The Star*, 23 December 1991.

Legum, Colin, " South Africa : The way forward", *New Africa* (London), No. 283: April 1991, pp. 9-11.

Lehulere, K., "Building a mass-based Patriotic Front", *Mayibuye* (Marshalltown), Vol. 2(6)., July 1991, pp. 35-38.

Makwetu, Clarence, "PAC unbending over 'struggle", *Saturday Star*, 28 December 1991.

Moolla, Moosa, "Significance of the contribution of India to the struggle against apartheid", *Notes and Documents* (New York, U.N. Centre against Apartheid), No. 17/76: July 1976.

Nannan, Sukhwant Singh, "South Africa's changing political scenario", *Strategic Analysis* (Delhi), Vol. XIII (iv): July 1990, pp. 443-52.

Padgaonkar, Dileep "Apartheid under fire : Racist regime at cross-roads", *The Times of India*, 2 January 1990.

Pheko S.E.M., "Statement of the Pan Africanist Congress of Azania (S. Africa) at the 47th session of the UN Commission on Human Rights, Geneva", *Azania News* (Dar es Salaam), Vol. 27 (7): Jan.- March 1991, pp. 35-38.

— ,"Constituent Assembly no substitute for armed struggle", *Azania News*, Vol. 26 (9): July - Sept 1991, pp. 28-29.

Ramamurthy, T.G., "The world campaign against apartheid: A new dimension", *Ind-Africana* (Delhi, University of Delhi), Vol. II (I): April 1989, pp. 21-27.

Sawant, Ankush B., 'The organization of African unity and liberation struggle", *Africa Quarterly* (Delhi), Vol. XXV (3-4), pp. 36-44.

Saxena, S.C., "Apartheid -crime and its collaborators", *Ind-Africana,* Vol. II (1) : April 1989, pp. 1-20.

— ,"Indians abandoning ANC in S. Africa", *The Times of India,* 22 January 1992.

Schlemmer, L., " Theories of plural society and change in South Africa", *Social Dynamics,* Vol. 3(1): 1977, pp. 3-16.

Sidler, Peter, "South Africa : The rocky road to reform", *Swiss Review of International Affairs* (Zurich), Vol. 33 (1): March 1984, pp. 27-31.

Singh, Harjinder, "Winds of change in South Africa", *The Hindustan Times,* 13 March 1990.

Sparks, Allister, "Civil war: Cycle of revenge and retribution", *The Times of India* , 20 September 1990.

— "The sinister 'third force' in South Africa", *The Times of India,* 19 September 1991.

Spence, J.E., "South Africa: Reform versus reaction", *World Today* (London), Vol. 37 (12): December 1981, pp. 461-68.

—,"Reform in South Africa - a tangled web", *Contemporary Review* (London), Vol. 244 (1416): January 1984, pp. 6-15.

Stoffel, Vandermerwe, "The Nationalist Party's reform programme", *Africa Report,* March/April 1986.

Thomas, Susan, "Yes, carry on Mr. De Klerk", *The Times of India,* 22 March 1992.

Tutu, Desmond, "Referendum was a racist slap", *The Hindustan Times,* 23 March 1992.

Venkatsubbiah, H., '"India and the apartheid question", *India Quarterly,* Vol. XXXIII (1) : Jan. - March 1977, pp. 62-70.

Vohra, Ruchita. "De Klerk's liberal credentials are suspect", *The Times of India,* 6 September 1989.

Waldmeir, Patti, "South Africa : the unthinkable starts to look inevitable", The Times of India, 6 January 1990.

Woods, Gavin, " Towards a new constitution for South Africa : why the IFP rejects a Constituent Assembly", *Clarion Call,* Vol. 1 : 1991, pp. 12-15.

Woodward, Calvin, "Reform or revolution in South Africa", *Round Table* (London), No. 282 : April 1981, pp. 101-15.

Yollenhoven, S., "South Africa at the cross-road", *Third World Quarterly* (London), Vol. 8 (2): 1986.

Books

Adefuge, Ade, *Culture and Foreign Policy : The Nigerian example* (Lagos, Nigerian Institute of International Affairs, 1992).

Alden, Chris, *Apartheid's Last Stand : The Rise and Fall of the South African Security State* (London, Macmillan Press, 1996).

Aluko, Olajide and Timothy M. Shaw, eds., *The Political Economy of African Foreign Policy* (London, Gower Publishing Company, 1984).

–,ed., *The Foreign Policies of African States* (London, Unwin Brothers Ltd., 1977).

Barber, James, *South Africa's Foreign Policy* (London, Oxford University Press, 1993).

Barratt and James Barber, eds., *South Africa's Foreign Policy : The Search for State and Security 1945-1988* (New York, Cambridge University Press, 1990).

Brewer, John D., ed., *Can South Africa Survive* (London, The Macmillan Press Ltd., 1989).

Chhabra, Hari Sharan, *South African Foreign Policy : Principles-Options-Dilemmas* (New Delhi, Everest Press, 1997).

Cope, John, *South Africa* (New York, Frederick A. Praeger, 1967).

Hunter, Jane, *Israeli Foreign Policy : South Africa and Central America* (Boston, South End Press, 1987).

Jaster, Robert Scott, *The Defence of White Power : South Africa's . Foreign Policy* (London, Macmillan Press, 1988).

Lyman, Princeton N., *South Africa's Promise* (Washington, Carnegie Endowment for International Peace, 1996).

Macfarguhar, Roderick, ed., *The Politics of China 1949 -1989* (New York, Cambridge University Press, 1993).

Martin, David and Phyllis Johnson, *Apartheid Terrorism* (London, Villiers Publication, 1989).

–,*Destructive Engagement* (Zimbabwe, Zimbabwe Publishing House, 1986).

Marquard, Leo, *The People and Policies of South Africa* (London, Oxford University Press, 1962)

Safran. Nadav, *Israel: The Embattled Ally* (Cambridge, Harward University Press, 1978).

Saxena, S. C., *The Foreign Policies of African States* (Deep and Deep Publications, 1982).

Stein, Leonard, *The Balfour Declaration* (New York, Simon and Schuster, 1961).

Stevens, Richard P., *Weizan and Smuts : A Study in Zionist South African Cooperation* (London, The Institute for Palestine Studies., 1975).

Thompson, K. W., ed., *Foreign Policies in World of Change* (New York, Harper and Row, 1963).

Thomas, Scott, *The Diplomacy of Liberation: The Foreign Relations of the ANC since 1960* (London, I. B. Tauris, 1996).

Articles

Aardt, Maxi Van, "A Foreign Policy to die for: South African response to the Nigerian Crisis", *Africa Insight* (Pretoria), Vol. 26 (2) : 1996.

Adelman, Kenneth, "The Club of Pariahs", *Africa Report* (New Brunswick), Vol. 25 : November-December 1980.

Bischoff, Paul-Henry, "South African Foreign Policy under a democratic Mandela government", *Indian Journal of African Studies* (Delhi), Vol. VIII (1 & 2): April & October 1997.

Crawford, Neta C, "South Africa's New Foreign and Military Policy : Opportunities and Constraints", *Africa Today* (Denver), Vol. 42 (1 &2): 1995.

Essack, Karrim "South Africa and Israel", *Liberation* (Denmark), No. 6 : November/ December 1986.

Evans, Graham, "South Africa in Remission : The Foreign Policy of an Altered State", *The Journal of Modern African Studies* (Çambridge), Vol. 34 (2): 1996.

Husain, Azim, 'The West South Africa and Israel : A Strategic triangle", Third World Quarterly (London), Vol. 4 (1 J.January 1982

Hunter, Jane, "Israel and South Africa : Two Comrades in Arms", *Middle East International* (London), No.250 : 25 July 1986.

–, "South Africa : Israel's friend in need ?", *Middle East International*, No. 348:14 April 1989.

Iheduru,. Okechukuv C. "Post - Apartheid South Africa and its neighbours : a Maritime Transport Perspective",*The Journal of Modern African Studies*, Vol. 34 (1):1996.

Mandela, Nelson, "South Africa's Future Foreign Policy", *Foreign Affairs* (New York), November-December 1993.

Milazi, Dominic, 'South Africa's Foreign Policy in the Post-Apartheid Era : What are the key international issues", *Indian Journal of African Studies* (Delhi), Vol. VIII (1 & 2): April & October 1997.

Mills, Greg, "Changing the guard : South Africa's Foreign Policy into the 1990s", Africa Insight, Vol. 20 (3): 1990.

—, "South Africa's International Relations under Mandela", *Indian Journal of African Studies*, Vol. VIil (1 & 2): April and October 1997.

Moleah, Alfred T., "The Special Relationship", *Africa Report*, Vol. 25 : November- December 1980.

Sachs, Bernard, "South Africa : Life on a Volcano : The Jewish Community in a caste society", *Commentary* (New York), Vol. IX: June 1950.

Index

T

U

V

W

Z